# The Case of the Cast Iron Dog

## Gene Zimmerman

For information contact
Publius Press
4900 Penrose Dr.
Newburgh, IN 47630
Book design: Michael Austin
ISBN-13: 978-1548958923
ISBN-10: 1548958921
10 9 8 7 6 5 4 3 2 1

# The Case of the Cast Iron Dog or You Can't Teach an Iron Dog New Tricks

by
Gene Zimmerman

Edited by
Kathryn Duncan

*Special thanks to Jessica Miller and Michael Austin for help in preparing this manuscript*

# *Editor's Note*

Either directly or indirectly, I owe much of my professional success to Gene, whom I think of as my adopted dad. He found the funds for me to fulfill my dream of going to the University of Florida, and he inspired my dissertation on eighteenth-century British pirates as well as later work on Methodists. Gene always said the great part about adopting each other is that we didn't have to carry with us any baggage or hurtful history. The best part, in my opinion, is feeling chosen, of feeling that Gene wanted to adopt me, and I'm eternally grateful for that. I'm happy to be able to collaborate with Gene.

This collection is a reprint of Gene's original book, *Why Do Mullet Jump?*, published in 1986, with the addition of previously unpublished and new works, including essays on gay marriage and the Pulse nightclub shooting. We hope you enjoy visiting some of Gene's greatest hits and reading some of his new thoughts. You will find profound wisdom in all as well as humor and a warm, authentic voice.

# *Author's Note*

When I, Gene Zimmerman, was assigned to my second church, I inherited a weekly church newsletter and in it "The Pastor's Page." That meant I had to write something to the congregation every week. Looking to see what the former pastor had said, I found it was mostly about the financial needs of the church, their lack of attendance, and things like that. I determined not do the same. Instead, I decided "The Pastor's Page" would be something about our faith, human events in which I saw God involved, or some of the struggles we go through trying to be Christians—things of that sort. I hope you discover such things in this book. It would make me very happy.

Upon being appointed to Southside United Methodist Church in Jacksonville, I soon came to know a very sharp young student named Kathryn Duncan. Several things soon brought us together. One was that she payed close attention to the sermon and another that she had a life long desire to be a Florida Gator. Being the preacher and having graduated from the University of Florida made that first meeting easy and interesting and led to a lifelong friendship. Here we are now; I'm retired and still writing stories (for the fun of it), and here she is Kathryn Duncan, Ph.D. and English professor at Saint Leo University in Florida, and we are collaborating on a book. What fun!

*Gene Zimmerman*

# *You Can't Teach an Iron Dog New Tricks*

Down the street from where we once lived was a life-size cast-iron dog that stood watch over a two-story house. We became so attached to him that we named him "Ironsides," and our daughter would shout and wave at him as we went by. He didn't seem to notice her or, if he did, gave no indication of it.

"Ironsides" was an admirable bulldog and represented the highest loyalty of his breed, for he guarded the house night and day letting nothing alter his stance: not a bone, not a lady dog, not even a well-placed kick. He was a veritable Gilbralter.

I like that kind of loyalty. It was both comforting and encouraging to pass by and always find him at his post. However, one thing spoiled this picture of perfect loyalty—"Ironsides" was hollow inside! He stood there because someone poured him in a cast, placed him in a fixed position, and brought him to rigid attention in the front yard. I don't suppose, when you consider this, that you could call him loyal, since he really didn't have any choice in the matter.

God could have molded us in a fixed position and pointed us in a particular direction, but like "Ironsides" we'd be hollow inside.

Good is only good when a person has the choice of doing evil. Love is only love where the possibility of hate exists. God took a terrible risk giving us wills of our own, but that's the only way we can ever be truly alive. What a joy it must be to God, who took this risk, when we choose to be loyal, to be steadfast, to be loving, to be good.

# A Link in the Chain

A few years ago, on a small island in the south east Bahamas, a dream came true for a lady who lived there. Her name was Mrs. Myrtice Brown, and her dream was to someday build a home there to care for small children who had no home.  Long before her dream came true, both she and her daughters would make a place in their own homes for such children.  I remember going to the island once and seeing the older daughter with several small children in tow. That's when I learned the story.

A couple years had passed when a group of us got together in the minister's residence to see how we could make "Miss Myrtice's" dream come true. Before we left that day, the land and labor had been given and enough money to get started.  Today, Zion Home is in full operation, and it is the result of many hands and hearts and gifts.

Now let me bring you up to last Monday.  A sewing group in Okeechobee heard about the home and made a personal quilt for each child.  It was to be each child's own, they said, so that every child could have something that belonged to him or her.  Their large box of quilts  was sent to me to keep until another private plane came through on the way to Zion Home.  The day arrived, and I loaded them on a large push cart to get them over to the church, our staging area.  The only problem was that I couldn't get the large box through the double doors of the place where I live.  I was holding a door open with a foot, the other door with one hand, and trying to pull the cart through with the remaining hand. ( Visualize that if you can). Just as I was finding this arrangement wouldn't work,  the foot-held door suddenly opened wide.  Turning around, I saw a young woman in running attire holding the door open.  She hardly said a word and, when I got through the door, ran on.  I wanted to thank her more appropriately and maybe learn her name, but she was gone.

On the way to the church, I was thinking about her "random act of kindness" and  how she had been an anonymous link helping the quilts get to the children. Such thoughts made me want to tell you this story and what I think it means. Her small, momentary act of help had a much more meaningful end than she could imagine: It assisted in getting quilts to the children in Zion Home in the Bahamas. Secondly, I believe this is one of God's ways of linking small acts of good will together until the larger result becomes far more significant. Lastly, don't pass up the smallest chance to help. Who knows what God's going to do with it?

# The Habits of Quail

I was trying to concentrate but somehow couldn't. The sermon was a little too soothing and, instead of holding your attention, lulled you to sleep. I began to slip into a state of neutral resignation when suddenly a sharp, shrill sound cut through that dreamy reverie, and my attention jumped up and fled outside. For the next twenty minutes, I listened to the sermon that was being preached out there.

The sound came from a quail who was hidden somewhere close in a tall clump of grass or palmetto patch. "Where are you?" "Where are you?" "Where are you?" he said. That's what a quail always says when he whistles. In fact, I think that's the only reason he whistles. Either the covey has been scattered and he's trying to find the others, or, as in this case, it is mating season, and he was calling to his mate. In either situation, the question is, "Where are you?"

He whistled for five minutes, ten, twenty, stopping at intervals to listen for a reply. "Where are you?" he called, and finally the answer came. "Over here! Over here!"

If you know the habits of quail, you can visualize the drama that begins to take place. For a moment or two, the call goes back and forth to determine where the other is, and then they begin running toward each other, stopping at intervals to call again. After a few minutes, all is quiet, and you know they are together.

Such was the case in the field outside the chapel where we were sitting, and I thought about God. The prophet said that God whistles (Isaiah 7:18). "Where are you? Where are you?" God says, and there is only silence. Again and again, God calls, and no one answers. Finally a reply is given, "Over here! Over here!"

Then each begins to proceed toward the other, pausing to say, "Where?" "Here!" "Where?" "Here!" After some interval, we make our way toward each other, and the calls cease. We have met and found one another.

Our hope lies in the fact that God keeps calling to us over and over, calling and listening. Our salvation is in the reply: "Over here, over here," and then in making our way toward God, calling and listening. It is God's calling that makes us aware of God's presence; it is our response that brings us together.

# *Advice for Beginners*

I feel sorry for the beginning golfer who joins a foursome that's been at it a little longer. There are always one or two who take special delight in telling him how to play. They watch the stance, the grip, the swing and come forward with all kinds of advice on how to do it properly. (Oftentimes the "advisors" aren't that good themselves, but, having passed the starting point, they are eager to come back to help the beginners. There seems to be some special pleasure in it.)

"Keep your head down." "Close your stance." "Change your grip." I've heard all those at the same time, and once, just as the fellow was about to swing, somebody hollered "Relax!" Now how can anyone possibly relax with all of that?

Sometimes it must feel that way to the beginning Christian. "Do this." "Do that." "Read your Bible." "Believe this." "Don't believe that." "Pray." I know from past experience how confusing all this can be.

Of course, we can't do it entirely on our own. We all need guidance and direction from those who have gone before us. This is one of the purposes of the church. In the end, however, we have to proceed on our own way, following the inner leading that God gives to those who seek God.

This is not an effort to have you ignore the advice of others; it is, rather, an attempt to say that your own judgment and experience are trustworthy even though you may have just begun. St. Paul said God's spirit bears witness with our spirit that we are the children of God. If God does this, then surely our own inner directions and decisions, guided by God's spirit, will be of primary importance.

# *Writing Notes in Church*

Some interesting notes turn up in the pews after church is over. I used to keep funnier ones but gave up after a while. It's not uncommon to find a bulletin left in a hymnal with something like this: "Do you love George? No. Then why do you go out with him? Nobody else has asked me." Of course, this one betrays the writer fairly easily. Once in a while, there's an offering envelope with a note on the back that says, "Isn't he ever going to quit?" Now and then, there's a message that is probably passed from one spouse to another: "He's talking about you."

Here's one that turned up in the offering plate one time. It, too, betrayed the writer's age and interest. It said, "I like church."

Underneath these words was a name signed in the same bold hand. Most of the notes are funny; this one warmed my heart. Somewhere in the congregation, there was a small child who was just learning to write. She liked the Sunday service and wanted to tell someone about it.

I thank God for this child. I am grateful that she found joy in being there even though she might not understand it all. I am thankful that a happy heart is open to God and waiting to have God speak to a growing and eager life. As for me, whatever time and energy it takes to prepare the worship service is worth it and more just to know that such a person is there.

Is it true a little child shall lead them? Perhaps more true than we know.

# *A Clasp of Hands*

He kissed my hand, not in a casual way but with much emotion and as though there was something sacred about it. I had asked if he would like to have a prayer, and he replied by extending both his hands to clasp mine and then, afterwards, to kiss it.

He was an elderly man from out of town, and I had been asked to call on him at the hospital. When I entered his room the first time and told him who I was, he said, "Praise God, you've found me."

We prayed that day, and he held my hand to his forehead during the prayer with profuse thanks afterwards for "finding him." Something about him made me think of Simeon: "This man was righteous and devout, looking for the consolation of Israel. . ." (Luke 2:25).

I'm not accustomed to people showing unusual deference to me as a minister. In earlier days, I didn't want people to think me "different." Now I know that I'm not different and don't think I deserve praise that belongs to God. So, for a few moments, I didn't know what to think about the man who kissed my hand. I knew it was an act of devotion on his part, but I didn't know how to receive it.

Afterwards, I stopped in the waiting room and looked out across the river for several moments thinking. It was not my hand that meant so much to him but the hand of God! It was God's hand that he was reaching for when he clasped mine. It was the blessing of God that came to us both when two human hands clasped in prayer. That's what it was; I'm sure of it. My hand is no more sacred than his, but something happens when two hands join to call upon God, especially where there is great need.

I left thinking that I won't mind being set apart, being different, if it could mean being a channel of grace for someone else and if, by our clasped hands, the hand of God would hold us both.

# *A Prayer for Survivors*

Today, I prayed for the survivors of the Nazi concentration camps. The prayer was prompted by the reading of an inscription found on a cellar wall where Jews had been hiding. It said, "I believe in the sun even when it is not shining. I believe in love even when I do not feel it. I believe in God even when God is silent."

Reading those words led me to sense some of the feelings of the one who wrote them—feelings of fear and faith, dread and hope, and who knows what else.

Did the writer die in that cellar, or did she or he go on to a concentration camp? Did the person die in the camp or survive?

If the writer died, his or her agony is over. If she or he survived, it isn't. That is when I felt an overpowering need to pray. I said, "O God, for all of those who have died from the inhumanity of others, I pray they may now be living in that perfect love, perfect peace, and perfect freedom that are yours. For those who have survived but remember such inhumane and unspeakable acts, I pray you will soften those terrible memories. May they not be awakened by nightmares that are true. May they have found friends and family for those who were lost, not to replace them, but to bring a new love and security that those dear ones cannot now give. God, I pray for all who have survived brutal and inhumane treatment, for they bear scars in body and mind that will not go away. I pray this prayer in the name of our Lord Jesus whose body bore the marks of human brutality. May he, who chose to suffer with all who suffer, bring comfort and peace to these for whom I pray. May I not forget to pray again and again and be brother to those whom I lift up before you today. Amen."

# *Peek out the Window*

The newspaper carried a story of an emergency landing at Dulles Airport in Washington D.C.. A large commercial plane couldn't get its landing gear down and had to skid in on its underside. Fortunately, no one was injured.

One of the passengers, a popular football star, said the pilot asked him to do three things: secure the door, keep the passengers calm, and, as the plane was landing, lower his head and not look up. He said he did the first two but had to peek out the window as they came down. "I figured if I was going to die," he said, "I was going to get a last look at the world."

I would think that a last look at the world would be intensely sweet. It would be free of petty irritations of all kinds. Even the big things wouldn't matter anymore—those past and present wounds that hurt and hinder our best living. All would be gone in the realization that this was the last look. The trees, the houses, the people, all would be beautiful as they went by for the last time.

If such things would be put in instant perspective when seen for the last time, why not do it now? Don't wait for the last look when there's too little time to rejoice and revel in them.

# A Quarter's Worth of Silence

We stopped at a nice sandwich shop during our summer travels and were enjoying our food when the juke box blasted forth. It was so loud, in fact, that we could hardly hear each other. After several minutes and a number of songs that all sounded alike, my wife, Emily Ann, said, "I sure wish you could buy a quarter's worth of silence on one of those things."

That, as a matter of fact, is an excellent and marketable idea. If the record companies would put a blank on each juke box, there are plenty of people who would gladly pay a quarter to keep from having their eardrums hammered while eating.

As we left, a big, brawny fellow walked in carrying a radio the size of a suitcase, and that dear wife of mine said to him in a sweet way, "I can see where you got all those muscles, carrying your radio."

Both of her statements are a commentary on our present day and the need of many people for constant sound. Silence is a rare commodity so much so that a lot of people don't know what to do with it. We're uncomfortable with others when the conversation stops, and someone invariably says something, even if it's silly. We leave radios and televisions on all day and half the night because being in a house alone seems eerie. The walkers, runners, and bikers wear earsets, and—would you believe—you can now get a pair for under water!

Silence is rich and lovely. It's a place to meet and talk with yourself. It is a time to hear the sounds of nature—such as beetles boring into the pine trees and squirrels gnawing the cones. It's a time when God can be met and more clearly understood.

The Bible tells us, "Be still and know that I am God." That's a call to get away from the noise and listen to the lovely sounds and voices of silence. Try a quarter's worth to begin with; after that, I'm sure you'll want more.

# *Brief Encounters*

A rubber band landed on the windshield as I pulled up at the traffic light. There was a school bus next to me and a boy about eight or nine looking out the window to see how good his aim had been. I gave him a thumbs-up sign to show him he had hit the mark. He grinned, and so did I. The light changed, and we moved on.

The smile stayed for a block or two, and I felt good inside. What about? Having fun with a young boy. Meeting for a brief moment in a bit of play and saying with a smile that there was an important person on the other end of the rubber band.

All of this may sound simple, but it reaches deep places in the human spirit. It says you're a person of worth. It recognizes you for yourself, establishing your special identity, acknowledging your importance as a person. Somehow, when it's done freely and without pretense, there's a mystical "touching" of two people in which each gives something to the other and both feel better for it.

I shall never forget a homeless man with whom I spent a half day. That morning, someone had said to me, "Good morning, how are you?"

"I cannot remember," he said, "when someone last spoke like that to me."

We do not have to spend much time with a person, nor do we need to know them, to convey feelings of worth, interest, or affection. A simple greeting, a smile, a courteous gesture, or a moment of play is all that's needed. Anyone, in a moment's passing, can make another person feel glad to be alive.

# Greek Wisdom

I saw my first Broadway play on a trip to New York City last year. Of all the plays I might have seen then or any other time, I attended the one I would have chosen, *Zorba the Greek*.

I have long read and admired the work of Nikos Kazantzakis who wrote that story. Zorba was a real person who greatly influenced the young writer. Kazantzakis not only wrote this book about him, but many of his writings reflect Zorba's native wisdom and high-spirited life.

Anthony Quinn played Zorba on stage as he did in the movie. He fits the part so well that he is Zorba. Having read the story again and again, I was enchanted as those fine actors brought it to life. I sat in anticipation waiting for scenes and lines I knew were coming and was not disappointed when they came. Life, death, love, God, all are strong themes in Zorba.

There were many memorable lines to quote, and I scribbled several of them on my program. One in particular came straight from the heart of Zorba but out of the mouth of Quinn: "The only death we die is the death we die every day by not living."

Those words made me not want to kill one moment of time in fretful, depressive living but to savor each day with joy and give God thanks for it.

# *Laughter and Faith*

Laughter is something I've long enjoyed, and seeing the funny side of things has provided a lot of fun and pleasure. But laughter is a complex human response, and people laugh for many different reasons, not just because something is humorous. We laugh when nervous and sometimes to ridicule. We laugh in grief or to ward off fear. (I've done that.)

In a more serious side of laughter, there is an element of faith. I've discovered that people of great faith often have a delightful sense of humor. How do faith and humor go together? For one thing, those people are able to laugh at themselves. They see their own ineptness, and, instead of being embarrassed or exposed, they chuckle at themselves.

(I'm afraid a lot of our stuffy soberness comes from trying to act "all together" when no one really has it all together. People are funny to me when they try to act as though they don't make mistakes and then do. But don't laugh out loud at them; they get mad about it!)

Humor belongs to the faithful, also, because they know that whatever happens is not the last word. In the trusting man or woman is the belief that this event, though painful or tragic, is not the end. At the end is God and even now, within this experience, God is with us. As a result of this kind of faith, people have expressed gentle humor in their grief and still have the capacity for laughter when their burden seemed overwhelming.

One day I was having lunch with a friend for whom every movement is difficult because of a birth defect. After a particularly difficult time trying to drink her beverage, she said, "Well, one thing is certain, I'll never be a drunk. I can't get enough in me at one time." Her faith and humor have time and again lifted her above her difficulties.

There are several statements in the Bible about laughter, but the one I like best was made by Sarah who burst her sides when told she and her 100-year-old husband were going to have a baby. "God hath made me to laugh," she said, "so that all that hear will laugh with me" (Genesis 21:6, King James Version). And when her son was born, she named him Isaac, which means "he will laugh," for she knew that God had given her laughter and would offer it to her son as well.

# *Sending Messages*

To mark the fortieth anniversary of World War II, a book of poems, written by rank-and-file people, was published in Britain. The poems came from service men and women, factory workers, worried mothers and fathers, people of all kinds who wrote their thoughts and feelings during wartime.

One that I particularly liked was written by a young woman who sent messages from the shore to ships riding at anchor. Sometimes, she used flashing light, other times a telegraphed code. For several weeks, she was in daily contact with an American sailor on board one of those ships. After their official work was done, they began sending personal messages back and forth. Those signaled words created an affection between two people and a hope they would meet after the war.

The young woman's poem was a poignant story about a person she came to love but could not see. As I read it, I thought of God and faith in God. The messages seem so real. There is Someone there both sending and receiving. One day, we shall see face to face; for now, we must be content with the message and the faith that we shall meet.

# *Shouting 'Good News'*

The morning paper was heavy with war, atrocities, and famine, all in far-away places. At home, it was murder, rape, and child abuse. On the way to work, I was thinking about the first Christians referring to the life, death, and resurrection of Jesus as "Gospel"—good news. Then it struck me that you can't know how good that news is until you understand how bad the world can be and that it was against the backdrop of such a world that they shouted "good news" at the top of their lungs.

It was in the face of such things that Paul asked the question, "Who shall separate us from the love of Christ? Shall tribulation, or distress, or persecution, or famine, or nakedness, or peril, or sword?. . .No, in all these things we are more than conquerors through him who loved us. For I am sure that neither death, nor life, nor angels, nor principalities, nor things present, nor things to come, nor powers, nor height, nor depth, nor anything else in all creation, will be able to separate us from the love of God in Christ Jesus our Lord" (Romans 8:35, 37-39).

Here is the full recognition of the dark side of life, but in the face of it is the strong knowledge that "we are more than conquerors through him who loved us."

I do not want to shield myself from hearing the bad news. In fact, we should listen more carefully and feel it more deeply. Neither do I want to grow discouraged and despondent about it. Rather, when I hear it and have listened carefully enough to know its awful reality, I desire to shout aloud with our forefathers and foremothers, "Good news! Good news! Christ has come!"

# *Taking Our Blessings for Granted*

The story of healing of the ten lepers is a familiar one (Luke 17:11-21). They called to Jesus from a distance because they were forbidden to approach anyone. He called back to them, "Go and show yourselves to the priests." This, too, was a matter of law. No leper could return to the community until he or she had been examined by a priest and pronounced free of the disease. Luke tells us, "as they went they were cleansed."

You can imagine the pandemonium among them. Finding themselves healed, they ran toward the priest for examination—all but one, that is. One turned and ran toward Jesus "praising God with a loud voice."

"Were not ten cleansed?" Jesus said. "Where are the nine? Was no one found to return and give praise to God except this foreigner?"

The message is obvious, but I want to lift up one word for thought: foreigner. Nine were Jews; one was not.

It's surprising how often in the Gospels the truth is grasped by "foreigners," people who weren't too familiar with the religion around them. That has its parallel in the present, for it's often the foreigner who has to tell us what a great country this is. It's the outsider who sees how blessed we are to have work to do, a family to love, a church to serve, a God to thank.

When such things are so near, we often forget what a high privilege we have, how much we are blessed, how fortunate we are. "Foreigners" ought not to have to tell us these things; we should be telling them.

I suggest we take what is now considered commonplace—nation, home, work place, church—and make note of the wonderful gifts that are given to us through them. Then "praising God with a loud voice," give thanks.

# *Handwriting on the Wall*

It isn't often you find the larger questions of life dealt with on the walls of a public restroom, but such was the case at a convenience store located along Highway 98 in West Florida. In the midst of the scatological commentary, someone had written a theological statement: "God loves you." Another patron came along after that and wrote underneath, "And just what good does that do?"

It's refreshing to see such serious debate going on in a place like that. Had I not been in a hurry, I might have joined in.

I think I would have written, "Everyone needs love. Isn't it good that God loves us?" Next, I might have added, "There's nothing like the company of a loving friend." And then, "Those who love sacrifice because they want to give us their best."

Since all of these ideas are in the Bible, I would have written John 3:16 and been found out. Only a preacher would use three points and a text! The literary guild of outhouse authors would surely have taken off on that.

Perhaps it was best I didn't add anything so all who came in could answer for themselves when they saw, "God loves you." "And just what good does that do?"

# Why Do Mullet Jump?

No one seems to know why mullet jump. My guess is they do it for the same reason children skip, bear cubs tussle, or a young colt suddenly breaks and runs—just for the fun of it! Nature is very playful, and, if you watch for it, you will see many of its creatures running, jumping, diving, sliding, and swooping, just for the joy of it.

There is a great gaiety in the heart of God, for many things in the world appear to be here just for the fun of it. It wasn't necessary that flowers be colorful nor sound be arranged so as to be musical. It seems such things were created for God's pleasure as well as ours.

The German theologian Jürgen Moltmann says that God was "playing" when God created the world (*The Theology of Play*). Moltmann defines play as something one does not have to do but is free to do and does for the joy or pleasure of it. The book of Genesis bears this out when it reveals God's response to creation as "good" and "very good."

If God was having pleasure in creating the world and seeing to it that its creatures could hop, skip, jump, and be colorful, why can't we do these things, too, just for the fun of it?

A person doesn't have to be "useful" to be of worth, nor do we always have to do "useful" things in order to justify our existence. Our existence has already been justified by a God who, for the joy of it, said, "Let them be," and at the same time gave us many marvelous things to see and do just for the fun of it. Anyone for tennis?

# *Learning to Listen to Rock*

My son and I took a few days of vacation together one summer. It was one of those man-to-man things. He brought a friend, I met my brother down state, and we went on from there.

We left Jacksonville, Florida early in the morning, and the first thing that turned on after the engine was the radio—full blast. The station was ROCK 123 or some such. The day was warm, and the windows were up, and here we went entombed in that terrible cacophony of sounds.

If you're familiar with rock music, you know it is played at only one level—loud—and that it has a monotonous drum beat that repeats itself over and over—wham bam, wham bam, wham bam, etc.—until you are sure that fellow in the headache ad who pounds the inside of your head with a mallet is now a rock-and-roll drummer.

The lyrics aren't much more exciting than the beat. Most rock songs seem to have the words "all night" in them with the remaining ones rhyming in some way. For example, all night, wham bam, out of sight wham bam, just right, wham bam, extra light, wham bam, etc., ad infinitum. (If someone will set that to music, we'll make a million.)

After ten minutes of the music, I said to myself, "I will not be able to endure this for 150 miles. My brain will be mushy. The man with the hammer will bring 15 of his friends and beat it to a pulp by then." Next, I thought, "But we're off to have a good time together, to be close and more understanding. Perhaps I should begin by finding something to like in the things he likes."

I'm still not a rock-and-roll fan, but I can listen to it because he likes it, and since I like him, I want to pay attention to the things he cares for. All right! Out of sight! All night! No, not all night, just now and then during the day.

# Getting Our 'Second Wind'

Athletes talk about getting a "second wind," and runners speak of breaking certain "barriers." In enough instances, it is reaching a point when something inside says, "You're tired; you're hurt; why don't you quit?" But you push yourself past those voices and run faster or leap farther, and a game is won or a record set.

After it's over, there is a wonderful feeling of achievement, even of exhilaration, that you made yourself go on. There is also a sense of self-mastery for not listening to the complaining or quitting voices.

There is a carryover of this training into our common life. For some reason, we hear the same things when we're pressed up against something that calls for more effort. "Quit. . .Don't try. . .I'm hurt. . .Everything's against me. . .I can't do it." For some reason, as a youth, I felt this inner advice had to be heeded, so when I felt sad, I stayed sad until it went away of its own accord. If lazy, then I did nothing until energy returned.

Slowly, I began to say, "Hey, I don't want to listen to you. I'm tired of being sad, defeated, or tired. I'm going to break those barriers."

It isn't easy. You still may have to run while hurt or tired, but then that second wind comes, and you leave those things behind. When the goal is reached, there is a sense of achievement and, best of all, a feeling of self-mastery and control over all the defeatist words you heard.

Who tells me to quit? I think it's my "lazy self," the one who would rather play all the time, or my "feel sorry self," the one who says, "You're hurt. Why don't you curl up in a little ball and think of how sad it all is?"

To give in to those voices is to quit the race and never meet that strong masterful person who is so capable of going to greater self-knowledge and more exciting goals.

The apostle Paul had a lot to say about pushing on past discouragement and personal hardship. Here are a couple of his thoughts.

"I can do all things in him [Christ] who strengthens me" (Philippians 4:13).

"But thanks be to God, who gives us the victory through our Lord Jesus Christ" (1 Corinthians 15:57).

# *Simple Courtesy*

I was annoyed when the man, said, "You're welcome," because I hadn't said anything. He saw me hurrying to the elevator and held the door open. I was hardly in when he said, "You're welcome." He's chiding me, I thought, for not saying, "Thank you." At first I looked at the floor then decided to look at him. By this time, he had moved back and was facing another direction. That's when I saw the hearing aid.

Maybe he wasn't chiding me. Maybe he thought I had said, "Thank you" and wanted to be sure to respond. That's more likely what happened.

As we were leaving the building, I held the door for him and his wife. He smiled warmly and said, "Thank you." I smiled back and said, "You're welcome."

That brief encounter brought several things into focus. Because he thought I had thanked him or that I looked like someone who would, he wanted to respond in kind.

Discovery one: He assumed I was a courteous person and treated me as such. He honored me by that assumption. Discovery two: Because he thought me to be courteous, I made an extra effort to be so. Discovery three: What people think of us, we try to live up to. Discovery four: How contagious and influential a simple act of courtesy can be. It has the power to shape character even in a chance meeting with a stranger.

These thoughts about courtesy and assistance ended with Paul's words in Philippians 4:8: "Whatever is true, whatever is honorable, whatever is just, whatever is pure, whatever is lovely, whatever is gracious, if there is any excellence, if there is anything worthy of praise, think about these things."

# *Givers and Takers*

I know a lovely little country church that stands by the side of the road. It attracts people who pass by, and many stop to go in. Now and then, a note is found in the offering plate with a dollar or two. Now and then, the pump is missing, or a fan is gone.

What the passersby do when they enter that little church casts them into two sharp divisions: those who give and those who take away; those who care and those who don't; those who pray to God and those who prey on the things of God. I doubt the people who go in and out are aware that their actions define them so sharply, but they do.

In Jesus's parable of the last judgment (Matthew 25:31-46) a clear distinction was made among all who were there. The separation was between those who cared and those who didn't. That, according to the parable, is the sole determination of the judgment: whether you are for or against your brothers and sisters, whether you are here just to help yourself or to help anyone you can.

It appears that God doesn't judge us. We judge ourselves. God merely pronounces the judgment when the time comes.

# *Talking to God*

If you were talking with God and truly believed God was listening, would you stop, leave that sacred experience, and speak with someone else simply because that person called you? I did.

I felt a deep need to pray, not to ask for anything but to disentangle myself from two dozen things that were taking time and energy and not giving much back. That happens periodically, and, when it does, I have to sit quietly before God to find myself once more, put such things in perspective, and renew my spirit. This happens when you're alone with God, and you don't have to ask for it, though you can if you want. (I find the greatest gift of prayer is just being with God, not getting God to do something. If you've been with God, you can do the things you want done, or they may not even matter after that.)

If we asked God to be fully present to us, then we must also be fully present to God. This means we must unload a lot of baggage that we drag about every day. It means consciously removing ourselves from the surrounding world. It isn't that we "leave" the world; it is that the world doesn't define who and where we are at the moment. To do that requires some conscious preparation. You disengage yourself from time. You can't say, "It's now ten o' clock, and I've got to be somewhere else at ten-thirty." You also try to transcend place, that is, turn your attention away from the setting you're in with its sights and sounds and focus only on the desire to be with God.

Because of a deep desire to pray, I had done those things, or, rather, God had allowed them to happen. (God has never refused when it was my deepest desire or need.) I felt full; I possessed myself once more; I felt I was "above'" all the baggage I had left at the bottom of the mountain. At times like that, all I can say is, "Thank you, God, thank you, thank you."

It was then the phone rang. "This is absurd," I thought. "I will not leave God's glorious presence to answer the phone." It rang again, and I got up to answer it. The terrible incongruity of it all descended when I returned to pray. I had left God's presence and walked away to talk to an unknown caller simply because a bell rang twice. How can we possibly be with God if we are so tuned to every distraction that a ringing bell would call us away?

God waited for me. God waited for me while I talked on the telephone. I apologized and began again. God restored my soul!

I went back down the mountain and picked up some of the baggage—not all of it. I could now see some of it was junk and left it.

How can any of us learn to pray or worship if we have one eye on the clock and the other on something else? How can we ask God to be present to us if we are not fully present to God? There is joy in genuine prayer that exceeds all else. I know; I have experienced it. Today, I renew my vow that a ringing phone, a barking dog, or being too busy will not keep me from the most of all blessed human experiences, the company of God.

# Hospice Business

In a few minutes, I'll be leaving the church to go to the hospice board meeting. It's a business meeting but much more than that. What hospice is doing will so dominate our time and conversation that the financial reports will take their proper place—somewhere behind our purpose.

Sadly, many of the boards and committees I serve on are so tangled in the moaning and groaning about money that their meetings are more like wakes. At hospice, where we are literally preparing for a wake, there is an air of concern and accomplishment, even joy.

How can that be when we're dealing with death? The purpose of hospice is to help people who are dying to prepare for their own death. It is to make them physically comfortable and as spiritually real as possible. It also helps families care for their terminally ill members—a very important factor—and prepare themselves for the loss of a loved one.

Most people think that's a morbid task; strangely enough, it isn't. In facing death, people often discover life, life at its best, and for their remaining days savor its sweetness. Knowing the time is short, families are drawn together in a love that exceeds what they knew and a clarity of communication they never had before. And then, when the time comes, most hospice patients surrender their bodies without fear and with a faith and understanding that is rich and profound.

I must hurry or I'll be late for the meeting. I don't want to miss the blessing of being part of a caring ministry to the living and dying.

# *Finding the Gold*

It was said by a friend of Charles Williams, an English writer and publisher, "He found the gold in all of us and made it shine." What a wonderful talent to have and give, the ability to find something good in a person and lift it up for him or her to see and claim.

As a rule, gold isn't lying around in big chucks. It's mixed in with other stuff and has to be mined and refined, which means that most of us aren't able to see it that well in ourselves. It often takes someone else who cares enough to look for such talent (talent being a biblical measure of precious metal) and help us identify and own it. And what a joy it is to discover gold in yourself that you didn't know you had!

Of all those who do that, Jesus does it best. In fact, that's what God sent Jesus to do, "to find gold in us and make it shine."

# *Praying to the Crowd*

I have a growing annoyance with public prayers. Have you noticed how perfunctory many of them are? Since most are offered by preachers, this is an indictment upon us. What bothers me is that the prayer is not offered to God; it is spoken to the crowd. "Lord, we're here to work on this committee (as if God didn't know), and we ask that you help us to do our best. Amen." That's the short form. There are much longer ones that go with public dedications and, unfortunately, Sunday services.

Such prayers are usually crafted with the thought that the people will hear them. In truth, they should be prayed for God to hear and the people to overhear. That is the purpose of public prayer. The person who prays should address God on our behalf, gathering us up in the prayer and speaking with us and for us. When it is over, then we can all join in and say "Amen," which means "truly," "surely," or "I affirm what has been said."

Once, I had a terrible thought while listening to a prayer prayed to the crowd. I fantasized that I would say, "Lord, cover this man with leprosy and send all the plagues of Egypt on him for blowing this foul breath on us. Then heal him instantly before our eyes so he will turn to you only, gathering us up in his unworthy words to ask that we shall love you with all our heart, mind, soul, and strength. And if he or we will not do this, dear Lord, throw us in the lion's den and find someone you can trust."

Now that this has been said, I find myself indicted by my own complaint, which is often the case. I resolve, therefore, by God's help, to pray no longer to the people but to God alone. Will you join me and say, "Amen"?

# *Acting in God's Behalf*

One of the things I have learned through the years of the ministry is that God often aids us through other people. It has been my experience that when I had some personal problem or struggle that help would come—at a very opportune time—through some friends who, often, did not know how much they were needed or how much their kind acts accomplished.

As a pastor, I began to see that many times people were helped beyond what I tried to do or knew I could do. Their experiences led me to see and believe that God will move through and beyond us to assist other people if we are willing to act in God's behalf.

In reading Paul's letters, I'm impressed by the many people he mentions who were such bearers of God's grace. Here are a few: "We were afflicted at every turn—fighting without and fear within. But God, who comforts the downcast, comforted us by the coming of Titus. . ." (2 Corinthians 7:5-6). "I rejoice at the coming of Stephanas and Fortunatus, and Achaicus . . . for they refreshed my spirit. . ." (1 Corinthians 16:17-18). He said to Philemon, "The hearts of the saints have been refreshed through you" (Philemon 1:7), and of Onesiphorus, ". . . he often refreshed me" (2 Timothy 1:16).

It doesn't require a lot of knowledge of the right thing to do or say for God to use us in this way. It does require a concern for other people's need and a willingness to be used on their behalf.

The next time you try to do something good for God's sake, watch it out of the corner of your eye and see if more helpful things happened than you were able to accomplish by yourself.

# *The Experience of Easter*

The first time that Good Friday and Easter really meant anything to me was in 1946. I had begun a serious search for a faith I did not have and a God I did not know. A bulletin announced a special Good Friday communion at a church in Naha. Naha had been the principal city on the island of Okinawa—had been, because now there was nothing left of it. Hard fighting literally destroyed it.

On a hill overlooking the town was the church. It stood only because it was made of concrete with heavy thick walls. Even so, there were shell holes and bullet marks all through it. Riding through the rubble of the town and looking at the remains of the church, I knew something terrible had happened there. Nevertheless, the communion service was strong and comforting.

Easter sunrise service was miles away from where we were, and that meant getting up an hour before daybreak. Transport trucks were made available, and several left from our base. By the time we were on the road, others joined until it became a large military convoy. M.P.'s and S.P.'s were directing traffic. No one said much. On arriving, hundreds of men as gray shadows moved silently up the hillside.

The service began, and we sang a hymn, a chaplain prayed, another spoke. Then it happened. The sun came up out of the vast Pacific before us, and those grey shadows became men and were bathed in bright, radiant sunlight! I had a feeling of awe and mystery as though something profound was taking place.

There was not much I knew then about the death and resurrection of Christ, but as I look back now, I know the feelings were correct; a terrible thing took place on Good Friday, and something marvelous happened on Easter morning that left us bathed in a great light. Knowing more now than I did then, I still want to keep those first feelings as I relive the Easter season once more.

# *Caring for Each Other*

When I was eight or nine years old, my mother took me on a shopping trip to Tampa. We had returned to the car, and, remembering one more thing, she told me to wait there for her. The day was hot, so I stood beside the car. On the corner, a few feet away, was a boy about my age with a shoe shine box in his hand. While I was looking at him, he suddenly fell to the sidewalk as though something had struck him. The shoe polish clattered to the sidewalk and rolled in the street. A man who was standing near bent over him. Soon the boy got up and began to gather the contents of his shoe box. The man helped him. The light changed, and the boy left hurriedly.

It was a disturbing sight to me, and I told my mother all about it when she returned. She said the boy probably had epilepsy and tried to explain it to me on the way home.

That scene is still very vivid in my mind. I can close my eyes and see the car and myself, the boy and the man. I believe I might even find the corner. What I see so clearly is the pained expression on the boy's face. It was not physical pain. It was one of great embarrassment. It was there as he hurried away.

And the man who helped him, he, too, I clearly recall. I cannot see his face like the boy's, but I remember how gentle and kind he was in helping him up and can still see the two of them gathering the cans and the brushes.

We know more about epilepsy now and can control it better, and chances are that boy lives a normal adult life. But the remembrance of that day told me then, in a way I did not understand, and tells me now, in a way that I do, that we must care for and help each other. No one is exempt from suffering, and all of us, one day, will need others to care for us. Without someone like the man on the corner, we simply lie where we fall. I am deeply grateful there are many people like him. It is the way of God, and it is the will of God.

# *All in Good Time*

There is an old English charm that says:

"From Ghoulies and ghoosties,
  Long leggety beasties
and things that go bump in the night,
  Good Lord, deliver us."

I thought of those lines the other evening while listening to a speech. Suddenly, something went "beep" and then repeated itself several times around the room. It even happened near the speaker, and I saw him reach in his sleeve to shut himself off, from beeping, that is.

It was distracting to sit in an otherwise attentive audience and periodically hear that noise. That's when I thought of the above rhyme but changed it a bit to say "from things that go 'beep' in the night, Good Lord, deliver us."

I have a struggle with time, as some of you know. I don't want to be a slave to it, nor do I wish to cut my life into small segments and be forced to move on just because the clock says so. I realize, of course, that society would fall into chaos if this notion were taken too far, but sometimes I think we are driven by time much like the white rabbit in Alice in Wonderland who was forever rushing around, looking at his watch and exclaiming he was late. It's what we do inside the segments of time that is important, not marking them.

People who are having a good time forget time. That's why teenagers can honestly say, when dragging in late, "I forgot what time it was." While we want and need to be punctual, we should be more concerned about the quality of life that goes on in those periods rather than chiming in and hurrying on.

Life everlasting was not an appealing thing to me until I became aware that while you are genuinely enjoying yourself there is no awareness of time. If, then, in the company of God, we were "lost in wonder, love, and praise," we wouldn't know or care what time it was. Eternal life, therefore, is timeless. After that realization, I was willing to go.

# Getting Things 'Just Right'

In my last church, I had an office chair that I never seemed able to adjust just right. The tension was either too loose or too tight, so I got in the habit, when leaning back, to reach down and give the screw a turn or two to get the proper adjustment.

One day, I leaned back, gave it a quick turn, and fell over backwards! I had fiddled with the chair so much it finally fell apart.

The unexpected fall and knock on the head started me thinking. Said I to myself, "That's the way a lot of us do with our life; we keep fooling with it, trying to get everything 'just right,' until one day it comes apart."

I'm not sure God puts us here to do everything "just right." If so, most of us are poorly equipped for perfection. We come closer to understanding ourselves when we can see and accept some of our human limitations.

This isn't an invitation to pass off every failure by claiming imperfection or to avoid trying, but rather it is advice that we need to accept some imperfection and acknowledge that we can't do it all right all the time.

The encouraging thing about this reality is that God loves us and meets us at these places of imperfection with grace and strength.

# A Story of Two Sisters

The story of Mary and Martha is often treated in such a way that you have to choose one side or the other—usually Mary's, for she was listening to Jesus while her sister was rattling around in the kitchen trying to get lunch ready and complaining about the lack of help (Luke 10:38-42). But the more I read, the more I'm on Martha's side and the more I believe the story is not in the Bible to make a distinction between faith and works. No, it simply reveals two different types of people, how they express their faith, and the strengths and weaknesses of each.

Since I'm more on Martha's side, I'm going to try to vindicate her first. The scripture begins, "Now as they went on their way, he entered a village; and a woman named Martha received him into her house." Martha was one of those wonderful women who welcome people into their homes and go to work to serve them at their tables. (Food and hospitality are loving gifts that have rich spiritual dimensions. She understood this.)

We meet Martha again when her brother died (John 11). Once more, it was her strength that met the occasion. She had buried her brother and, on learning that Jesus was nearby, went to meet him. Here, she expresses a faith that was as strong as her character: "Lord, if you had been here, my brother would not have died." Jesus replies, "I am the resurrection and the life; he who believes in me, though he died, yet shall he live, and whoever lives and believes in me shall never die. Do you believe this?" She said to him, "Yes, Lord; I believe that you are the Christ, the Son of God. . . ."

Now this isn't a put-down of Mary, but since she's been treated as the better of the two, I wanted to get Martha on balance. However, Jesus commended Mary because she had the sensitivity to know when to listen. "One thing was needful," and she knew what it was: to stop and hear what he was saying. That's her great contribution—to tell us there are times when even necessary work has to be laid aside to listen to the Lord. And people who do that often hear things the "doers" miss.

At the outset, I said I thought this wasn't an "either-or" story but that it revealed two different approaches to life and faith. Such attitudes aren't necessarily chosen; they just are. What is helpful to remember is that both are important, and each needs the other. Weren't Mary and Martha lucky to be sisters?

# In God's Flock

Many of the words and images of the Bible are pastoral. They speak of sheep, grain, oxen, shepherds, farmers, barns, and vineyards. This poses a problem to translators when they carry the Bible into another language and culture. In some cases, the new readers have never seen or heard of such things as these, which are common to the Near East.

Such was the case of the Barrow Bible. Early missionaries, making a translation for the Eskimos, soon found that a lot of the biblical references were completely unknown to them. For example, the Eskimos had never seen or heard of sheep, so the translators used "wooly goats" an animal common to them. Consequently, Psalms 100: 3 reads, "We are his people and the wooly goats of his pasture."

I was amused when I read that verse, and my mind wandered back to those "wooly goats" in a few of the flocks I've tended. But with more sober reflection—and remembering that "All have sinned and fall short of the glory of God"—I reminded myself that there are very few sweet little lambs in God's flock, and the pastor could equally well be one of those wooly goats.

Perhaps the Barrow Bible is more nearly right when it says, "We are his people and the wooly goats of his pasture." And right now I'm grateful for the Good Shepherd who looks for the strayed and lost and is trying to bring everyone into the fold of God.

# *Disappointing Each Other*

We shall disappoint each other sooner or later, probably sooner. Even the people who know and love us best, especially them, we shall disappoint, for they have the highest hope and see the greatest possibilities in us.

It isn't that we want to do this. It is, apparently, part of our human frailty. Often we do so unknowingly, without thought or intent. But then some of our actions are conscious and willful. However you look at it, we disappoint each other. It seems unavoidable.

How shall we deal with such disappointment? By rubbing out the relationship? By looking at the other person as one who failed and therefore does not qualify for full trust? Shall we put an "X" on those who have disappointed us? But how can we when, deep down, we know we have done so ourselves?

Think of how God has dealt with us when we disappointed God. Has God said, "To hell with you!" or mark this as one who failed? (The only person God marked was Cain and that only as a warning to those who might harm him. It was a sign that Cain still belonged to God.)

No, God has refused to let our failures keep God from loving us or redeeming the relationship. It is the way of the cross. It is the refusal to let disappointment deter love.

Isn't our life enlarged when someone loves us beyond our callous ways? Aren't we left more sensitive and understanding when love and forgiveness refuse to go away because of some thoughtless word or deed of ours?

We must understand the way of the cross better and practice it more. By it, the deaf hear and the blind see, and through it, we receive and offer forgiveness. The forgiven know they are sinners and, therefore, find it easier to forgive.

# No Music, No Magic

There's a computer out there somewhere that has me mixed up with an address over on Beach Boulevard. I keep getting mail for "Rev. 4965 Beach Boulevar." I would feel a little better had it mistaken me for Simon Bolivar, the great Latin American emancipator, but, no, I'm an address on a misspelled street.

I can forgive a machine for not spelling my name correctly and even confusing me with the street, for, after all, it is only a machine. What is unforgivable is all those pretensions to personal friendship. "We have reserved for you, Rev. 4965 Beach Boulevar, three wonderful days, at the Rollickin' Resort," etc. etc.

The technology of our time is a marvelous thing and, if properly used, can be a great blessing to the world. Advances in medicine and agriculture alone can help us solve some of the great problems of health and food that confront us now, but they cannot do so without the human element. Machines must be programmed and made to work by human beings for the welfare of human beings. When used for exploitative purposes, machines can become our downfall!

A national magazine ran an article about the electronic production of music. It described what happens after an orchestra records a song. The machines can dissect it, add to it, and take away from it until the original is quite different from the music that is heard on the record. One of those electronic producers said, "All this equipment means you can do basically anything with sound. You don't even need musicians. But, without musicians, you'd lose the performance; you'd lose the feeling. You'd lose the only thing that has any magic to it."

Maybe that's why I don't like mechanical letters. There's no music, no magic, nobody on the other end.

# *Twice-Told Tales*

I could tell something funny was rumbling around in my friend when he started towards me. His eyes sparkled, and he was suppressing laughter, waiting for just the right time to turn it loose. He had a joke to tell and launched right into it. Just before he reached the "snapper," he stopped, his mirth subsided, and he asked, "Have you heard this one before?"

I had heard it, heard it, as a matter of fact, better told than he was telling it. However, if I said "yes," I would leave him with a crestfallen face and a limp, half-told story. If the answer was "no," it would be a falsehood. What to do? Quick as a flash, I said "no" and tried to laugh as hard as he did at the end.

Later, I consoled myself by saying I had not heard it before as he told it, and I began to wonder what God thought about things like that. Hasn't God heard it all before—the jokes, the complaints, the cries, the wants? Didn't Jesus say, "Your father knows what you need before you ask"? What if, when we started to pray, God said, "I've heard that a million times before and from you, seventeen"? Or, if with bright eyes and smiling face, we said, "Lord, the most wonderful thing just happened to me," and before we finish God said, "Yeah, I know it"?

God does know what we need before we ask, but what joy and delight God takes when we come to ask. It's in the coming, the opening of oneself to another, the desire to share something that we find meaning, not whether you know what someone is going to say before hand. It is the giving and receiving of ourselves that is so much more valuable than the prior knowledge of what is being said.

God may know what I'm going to say, but God wants to hear me and enjoy the way I tell the story. It's a new story when it's my story, and God likes to hear me tell it. (A special thanks to my friends who share my twice-told tales and still listen and laugh.)

# Love, Honor, and . . .Obey?

Whenever a prospective bride asks me what the wedding vows say, I smile to myself because I know what the next question will be: "Do I have to promise to obey?" "No," I reply, "that question hasn't been asked by the Methodist Church since 1910." (The Southern Methodists dropped it in 1910, Northern Methodists in 1864.) We usually laugh, and she says something like, "If I have to obey, I want him to obey, too."

I'm in sympathy with that concern and am glad we dropped the question long ago, for I believe marriage is a partnership of equals in which neither should have a subservient role to the other. As a matter fact, if we take those vows seriously when we pledge to love, comfort, and honor each other, there's no room for one person to hold authority over the other.

There is, however, a place for obedience in another relationship—the one we have with God. There, the vow could well be asked, "Will you love, honor, and obey?"

Obedience is an important part of faith. It is the recognition that God calls us to a way of life, a way that we understand enough about to say yes or no. To follow that way is to be obedient to it and to let God's call and command govern us.

Paul would tell the story of the Damascus road to validate his call from God. He told it at his trial before Agrippa and said to the king, "I was not disobedient to the heavenly vision. . ." (Acts 26: 19). Such obedience is our response of faith and trust in God and ultimately leads us to God.

# *The Gifts of Life*

The following statement is found in an excellent book by Arthur Gordon entitled *A Touch of Wonder*: "I felt that awful emptiness that comes from not knowing how much you love something until it is lost to you."

I marked those words and wanted to think about them some more. They point to the fact that we don't have anything permanently. Everything I call "mine" isn't mine in the sense that I possess it. So many things, including my life and the people I love, are not mine to keep. They are given for a while, and then I shall have to give them up. I could be bitter about it and curse the Giver for taking them back, or I could rejoice and thank God for the privilege of allowing me to share in this wonderful creation, which is marvelous and mysterious at the same time.

If one by one, I shall have to relinquish the gifts I have been given, including my life, I can live with dread and anxiety, fearing the time of separation and "giving up." Or, knowing these gifts are mine for a limited time, I can embrace each with joy, love them all as blessed gifts, and when the time comes to return them, say with gratitude, "Thank you."

Anyone who has lived a while knows "that awful emptiness that comes from not knowing how much you loved something until you have lost it." Maybe we have to pass through that experience before we learn that the time to love and enjoy something or someone fully is now. Then, when the time comes to say good-bye, we won't have to do so with such deep regret.

I would like so to live.

# Chosen People

The Jews know that being chosen of God does not mean being singled out for special protection or being given more of this world's goods than their neighbors. They were chosen to be bearers of God's word! They were chosen to live by and declare the knowledge that God had given them of both God's nature and will. Historically, their covenant with God has been costly. They have kept the faith, at times with great suffering to themselves. No one can say of the Jews that being chosen means being spared. That, obviously, is not the meaning of chosenness.

There is a dangerous doctrine floating about among Christians that, if they choose God, they will be exempt from suffering. Material gifts will be forthcoming, and God will ward off much of the evil that befalls others. This doctrine says in essence that good Christians lead charmed lives.

Not so! Christians often carry a heavier load. On the one hand, God may give them more because God needs the help and can trust them to do the job. On the other hand, Christians see people struggling and must reach out to take some of their burden.

But, if we don't get free passes through the world for being a Christian (or a Jew), then what do we get? The joy of doing God's work with God! The heart-stopping thrill of knowing, now and then, that God is close by. The surge of strength that infuses us when we discover that faith can conquer fear, even the fear of pain and death. That marvelous moment when we know we are not alone locked inside ourselves but that God is with us deep down inside our mysterious and uncertain selves.

We'd be better off not asking for exemptions (though I can't entirely keep from it) but asking only for the privilege of joining the faithful and doing well whatever God has given us to do, knowing that in this great company and through this task, we will find love, power, strength, and, in the end, triumph.

# *Dealing with Depression*

Someone, I do not now remember who or when, told me that he dealt with depression by picking out something he was thankful for and saying, "Thank you, Lord."

Anyone can get discouraged or depressed. Sometimes the feeling will even hang on like a bad cold that won't quite go away. When this happens, the days get gray, and the future doesn't seem much brighter.

At times, our feelings of depression take care of themselves; they drift off, and we're cheerful again. But, if depression lasts very long, we have to do something about it by taking ourselves in hand and working to overcome it (sometimes getting outside help).

I like that person's advice as a place to start: Find something you're thankful for and say, "Thank you, Lord." Do it more than once. Go through the day looking for things that bless and enrich your life and give thanks.

I see two important things this little exercise will do. It identifies the many good things that are all around us. Even if we are heavy laden, God does not leave us without daily gifts. This exercise also directs our attention away from ourselves and towards God and God's goodness. If we see evidence of God's grace and consciously turn to thank God several times a day, it's hard to stay discouraged because our attention is focused on God and not ourselves.

Try it; you'll like it.

# *Brotherly Love*

Jesus had four brothers and at least two sisters. We learn that from Mark's gospel when he tells about Jesus's return to Nazareth. "Is not this the carpenter, the son of Mary and brother of James and Joses and Judas and Simon, and are not his sisters here with us?"(Mark 6:3)

Reading that statement recently, it struck me that two of those brothers had the same name as two of Jesus's disciples—Judas and Simon.

Do you suppose he chose the two disciples because he had a prior affection for their names and attached it to them? That wouldn't be the sole reason, but I imagine it helped the decision. I have a predisposition toward anyone named Phillip because that's my brother's name.

It seems quite reasonable that Jesus would have a carry-over of affection and protection for those two disciples because that's the way he felt about his younger brothers Judas and Simon, whom he helped to raise. And when the disciples Judas and Simon betrayed him, it must have hurt all the more, for I doubt he ever erased the feeling that these two were his brothers.

He managed to save one. He forgave Simon and made him a leader again whom I trust he never thereafter betrayed. The other committed suicide and left him with an aching grief for a brother he loved equally well.

Frankly, I don't think that's the end of the story. I don't know how it ends, but I know that Jesus didn't stop loving Judas. If, as one form of the Apostles' Creed says, Jesus descended into hell, then I believe he went looking for his brother so they could all be together again.

# *Beautiful Weeds*

A weed appeared in the garden one day last year. It grew up among the azaleas, and I made a mental note to remove it. Before I got around to it, however, the weed became a big plant and put out a beautiful blossom. The large, white flower resembled the loudspeaker of an old gramophone and had a special beauty about it that far exceeded the common appearance of the plant.

It went away during the winter but is back now and trying to outdo itself with those gorgeous flowers. Four of them are just about to unfurl, and, as though it were planned for some special occasion, the flowers form a square on the outer edges of the plant. When open, they will appear as a beautiful floral arrangement on an elegant dining table.

It was the common appearance that fooled me. If there had been some exotic foliage or sign that said "astronomicus gorgiana," I would have expected more from the "weed" and been less harsh in judgment. I wonder if that isn't often the case with people?

# A Laughing Matter

An interesting interview was in progress when I flipped on the PBS station the other day. The announcer was talking with two people who conducted seminars on laughing. It seems that many people are too tied up to let go with a hearty laugh, and for the sake of such folks' good mental health and well-being these two were teaching laughing. (Shades of *Alice in Wonderland*. There the Classical master, an old crab, taught laughing in an undersea school that the Gryphon and Mock Turtle attended.)

The instructors on the radio said the seminars had to do with more than laughing. The number one fear of many people, they said, was fear of making a fool of themselves or appearing ridiculous before others. If these people could be taught to relax, to risk telling jokes and doing silly things, they would experience more inner freedom, less self-consciousness, and increased abilities.

All this may not be as much a laughing matter as it seems. A teaching hospital near me is conducting a one-day workshop on humor and health, and I'm going, because I, too, believe that laughter and humor are signals of something else. They reveal an internal faith and philosophy that make us more whole and wholesome.

One day when Brer Rabbit was about to be made into a stew by Brer Bear and Brer Fox, he burst into uncontrollable laughter. When asked what was funny, Brer Rabbit said he'd just remembered his laughing place. The other two wanted to see it, and, after much persuasion, he took them to a clump of bushes and pointed inside. In a moment, Brer Bear came out with a swarm of hornets behind him saying, "They ain't nothin' in here but a hive of bees." As he and Brer Fox took off with the hornets after them, Brer Rabbit was on the ground in a fit of laughter shouting, "I said it was my laughin' place and I'm laughin'!"

What's the point of all this? Find yourself a laughing place!

# Are You Listening?

We both spoke the same language, but she thought I said there would be two for breakfast and I thought I was ordering two scrambled eggs. The confusion came when she asked, "How many?" And I said, "Two," but her mind was on people and mine on eggs.

That little exchange is a good example of how easy it is to misunderstand another person. Both of us felt the question was clear and easily understood, but each was thinking something different. That probably happens more than we know.

Much more attention has been given to the speaking side of communication than to the listening end. We know how to talk, but we don't know how to listen. (I often suspect that in a group conversation, few people are listening; they're just waiting for their turn to talk. Just notice the number of times a speaker is interrupted and not allowed to finish.) Hearing is just as important as speaking and requires as much concentration, if not more.

Some years ago, I took a course in parenting. One thing I remember was "active listening." It meant focusing your attention on another so that you not only heard the person's words, but hearing past the words, heard their meaning.

Words are only symbols; we use them to convey meaning, and meaning can often be lost unless we look and listen for it. One of the best things about such careful listening is the feeling that someone is listening to me. She hears what I say and, consequently, understands and receives me. There is a deep and abiding need of human beings to be heard and received. We do this when we listen carefully.

Jesus said that God hears, understands, and receives us. What a blessed gift! Thank you, God.

# A Religious Nut

Scooped in between the other men on a limousine seat for two, I was trying to finish reading a book on the Gospels. I had an appointment to see the man who wrote it and wanted to finish it if possible. Consequently, I wasn't paying any attention to either of my companions.

It was the man on the left who got my attention. He was drumming nervously on his briefcase. I then glanced at the fellow on my right. His arms were folded tightly, and he was looking the other way.

"I bet they think I'm a religious nut," I thought. Here's this guy squeezed in between them reading a book on the Bible, and they can't move. So, one drums, and the other looks away. It was amusing, but I didn't laugh, just kept on reading.

I have a feeling that many people are more influenced by what others think of them than by what they think of themselves. Unfortunately, this starts early in life when we hear such things as, "You're dumb," "You're ugly," "You're bad," and we accept these judgments.

I doubt that any of us is totally free from accepting such opinions, but I want to be. I want to be governed by what God thinks of me and by what I think of myself rather than by the judgment of others.

So I kept on reading my book and thinking to myself, "Somebody on this seat may be a nut, but it's not me."

# In God's Name

The news carried a televised report of an ambushed train in El Salvador. It showed soldiers carrying bodies off the train and laying them on the grass alongside the track. Most were women and children. One was a girl who looked no more than thirteen. As they laid her body down, I saw, from the corner of the screen, a hand reach out and flip her skirt over her legs. It was a quick, almost casual movement.

The soldier who did it was no doubt trying to preserve her modesty and dignity even in death, but it struck me as a futile and almost incongruous gesture. Why, in God's name, didn't someone try to protect her dignity in life?

I know; I know! He didn't kill her; someone else did. But what we saw on that screen is happening all over the world. What we witnessed for a moment or two is something that can be seen daily somewhere on this earth. There are more than forty wars going on right now, and it is often the innocent who are the helpless victims. It appears that slaughtering civilians is a way to topple governments, so these mutilated bodies become a common sight.

Yes, it is a good thing to respect the dead by covering their bodies, but why not respect the living by protecting them and demanding the right for freedom to maintain the modesty of one's person?

I know that I should be saying this to the ones who killed the child, but, since I can't, I'm saying it to myself and to anyone else who will hear it: We must, in God's name, value human life so highly that we will never violate another person's life. Furthermore, we must vow, in God's name, to preserve every social standard that will allow children to have freedom, safety, and modesty.

Jesus said it would be better for a man to have a millstone around his neck and be cast in the sea than for him to offend a child. That's how important all this is to God. Somehow, we Christians must have a greater impact on the violence of the world. "Dear God, help us to find the way."

# *A Very Special Person*

I first met Tom one Sunday morning when leaving the house on the way to church. He had a Bible in his hand and was walking toward town. Since I was going that way, I offered him a ride. He was going to the Baptist church, which was across the street from ours. That was the beginning of a friendship that included several rides to town and an occasional drop-in visit.

On that first Sunday morning, after he got out of the car and started towards his church, he stopped, turned around, and said, "Some people say I'm retarded, and, if I am, that's O.K. I'm a very special person, and if they don't find it out, that's too bad."

The words struck deep, perhaps because he had said them about himself (usually someone else says such things), and because they were so clearly true.

Tom's words were true not only about himself but about everyone. There is a "special person" in each of us, and it is too bad when others can't see that.

Jesus had a way of seeing and speaking to those "special persons" and calling them out to become all that God wanted them to be: Zachaeus, the woman at the well, Mary Magdalene. No matter what the hindrance or handicap was, Jesus could see special persons and love them into a full life.

That's what God in Christ does for each of us, and we must do it for one another. It's our only hope. Start looking for the "special person" in people. Smile and speak directly to that inside person. What a joy and delight when that "special person" steps out from behind the outer appearance and greets you as one who recognizes who he or she is.

# *Naked before God*

Nikos Kazantzakis has written a rich and moving novel on the life of St. Francis. Though the book is fictional, many of the events are based on fact.

Francis was the reveling son of a prosperous merchant of Assisi who, after Francis's conversion, took him before the bishop to disown his son for fear Francis would dissipate the family income in alms and the rebuilding of churches. In answer to this, Francis took off all his clothes and lay them at his father's feet. Kazantzakis recreates this scene with these words:

"The Bishop descended from his throne, his eyes were wet. Removing his cloak, he wrapped it around Francis, covering his nakedness. 'Why did you do it, my child?' he asked in a melancholy, reproachful voice. 'Weren't you ashamed before these people?' 'No, Bishop, only before God,' Francis replied humbly. 'I am ashamed only before God. Forgive me, Bishop.'"

Most of our sense of shame and embarrassment is misplaced; it is concerned with what other people think. If it rested first in God, and we concerned ourselves with how God might look upon such a thing, we'd have little to be ashamed of before others and would find a clear guideline for life.

# *Making Great Music*

The man on T.V. held up two fingers and said that they were all that was needed to play "great, great music." He then turned to the electronic box he was selling and proceeded to peck out "Way Down upon the Suwanee River," calling to our attention that it sounded just like a banjo.

Wouldn't it be wonderful if you could make great music with two fingers and no more effort than that? Or would it?

Let's just say for the purpose of discussion that you can make great music with two fingers although anyone who's tried it with ten knows you can't. But say you could. Then what about the determination and devotion that was not needed or the love for great music that creates the incentive to start in the first place? They wouldn't be there. All the discipline that it took to achieve such skill would not be needed.

But aren't these the necessary ingredients to greatness? Aren't they the shaping influence? How can anything great come without devoted and diligent preparation?

The Christian life is not casual. Two fingers aren't enough; it requires all you have. We're shaped by the devotion and discipline we take upon ourselves. And, now and then when some disciple stands out among us as "great", we can be assured that he or she arrived there by a lifetime of love and practice.

Don't be discouraged that you aren't a "great" Christian. Very few are (and they would deny it), but, at the same time, don't be deceived that the hunt-and-peck system will get you there either.

# *Shootin' the Bull*

In the Navy, they call them "sea stories," and around the service station or truck stop it's called "shootin' the bull." It is, however, one and the same thing: telling tales about the past, usually yours, with considerable embellishment. If you've never done it, you ought to try it. It's a lot of fun. In fact, it's getting to be a lost art, because some of the better "shooters" are getting old and fading away and there aren't too many new ones coming on. It's that blasted T.V., I think; some people would just rather sit in a lump and stare at it than hear a good story teller stretch out a yarn. It's a poor imitation in my judgment.

In spite of my admiration and enjoyment of bull shootin', I am aware that all those stories are from the past—things that happened back then—and, if you aren't careful, you'll begin to think that all the really good and adventurous things happened back there. Both the teller and the hearer have to watch for that or they'll become nostalgic about a past that is gone and wasn't exactly as described in the first place.

Christians have to be careful about that, too. We tend to look back to the Bible days, telling those stories and thinking that the best of it all happened then. The Bible itself denies this. It says the greatest adventures are ahead, and it tells some marvelous tales about things to come.

"What no eye has seen, nor ear heard, nor the heart of man conceive, what God has prepared for those who love him" (1 Corinthians 2:9). Remember these words the next time you begin to think that all the good times are behind you.

# God's Surprises

Before attending one of our church's general conferences, I received a lot of mail concerning the issues that were before the body. Most of the letters expressed strong feelings and carried the names of many persons who signed a petition that was to come before us. This, of course, is the democratic way, and such correspondence helps a delegate understand the feelings of the church.

One letter, however, was different. The writer was offering prayers and encouragement to those of us who would represent the church. "I pray," he said, "that you will be open to the sovereign surprises of a mysterious God."

I like that statement. It helped me to keep in focus some important things that easily get lost in a large body of people trying to make legislation and chart directions for a church. Sometimes at the end of a long day when debate was heavy and contrary opinions sharp, you wondered what God had to do with this kind of human activity.

But then will come one of those "sovereign surprises;" a breakthrough would happen, a consensus would be reached, a decision would be made that contained more than our collective wisdom. "The spirit of God was moving. . .And God said, 'let there be light; and there was light.'"

Our faith is anchored in the belief that God entered the arena of human activity and works with us to accomplish the divine purpose. Regardless of how we may grope or struggle, if it is our will to do God's will, something will come of it. God will do more than we imagine or can do by ourselves.

Watch for those "sovereign surprises!" When you see one, say to yourself, "God is near." Such recognition and acknowledgement will lead you to see more surprises and to be closer to the God who gives them.

# *To Have and to Hold*

Rewriting the marriage ceremony was a popular pastime for a while. It's begun to subside now, and I'm glad. I'm not immovable about many things, but I am about that.

The first consideration is that the marriage ceremony is part of the church's liturgy, just as the baptismal and communion services are. Each one recites in carefully chosen language what we believe the significant events to be and what God gives us through them. These services belong to the church, not to the individual who asks to participate in them. Therefore, I explain that such ceremonies are not to be rewritten or restated unless the church itself chooses to do so.

Secondly, segments of the marriage ceremony are nearly a thousand years old. This means that for centuries the Christian church has been refining its faith and understanding about marriage. It has selected its words carefully seeking a beauty of language that is clear, concise, and strongly stated. It is highly unlikely that a couple would improve it by themselves any more than they could upgrade the Twenty-third Psalm or a Shakespeare play.

And lastly, I'm embarrassed to stand before a crowd of people to read some of the poor poetry and sloppy sentiment I've seen, most of which is focused on the couple themselves and not God or the great gift of marriage. Once a couple was so genuine and persuasive that I agreed to consider their liturgy. They had spent a lot of time writing and were certain I'd want to use it. I was to read it over, and they would bring a copy to the ceremony. It was as bad as any I'd seen.

In their haste to get to the wedding, they forgot that wonderful document! I said "Thank You, Lord," under my breath and asked them to repeat,

"To have and to hold, from this day forward, for better for worse, for richer for poorer, in sickness and in health, to love and to cherish, till death do us part, according to God's holy ordinance; and thereto I pledge thee my faith."

# *Uncle Bob's Box*

One summer in my hometown, one of the churches put on a Bible school under the direction of an evangelist who, as I remember, called himself Uncle Bob.

Uncle Bob had a number of relics and curiosities from the Holy Land. One was an olivewood gavel that, when he rapped on the pulpit, was supposed to command silence.

Among these things was a mysterious box said to contain some sort of strange and exotic object. If we came to Bible School every day, he promised to reveal its contents at the end. Each morning, he would take the box out and peek in with a great deal of awe and mystery. In addition, we were promised a big picnic on Saturday. With all these inducements, an earthquake couldn't have kept me away.

The box grew in size until it was as big as the church. The picnic promised to be just a shade short of paradise.

On Thursday, Uncle Bob announced that the picnic would be held in the school yard and everyone was to bring her or his own lunch. That cut my commitment in half right then and made me suspicious, but I felt it was worth coming one more time to see what was in the box.

I have forgotten what the box contained. All I remember was the disappointment that there wasn't anything in it worth going to Bible School for a whole week. I thought the whole thing was a fraud—Uncle Bob, the box, the picnic, and the church that perpetrated that hoax on all us kids. I never went back.

Later, I vowed never to deceive people about Christ and the church, nor would I bait them with any kind of promise save the privilege of meeting Christ. All by himself, Christ and his kingdom is a lovely thing. To cheapen that with deceptive technique and petty promotions is near blasphemy.

# *Love Is Like That*

I've just finished a funeral service for someone I didn't know, an elderly woman whose few remaining family members requested a Methodist minister. There weren't more than a dozen people there, and most were older. The exception was two children sitting on the front row, a boy of six or seven and a girl about eleven. No one there seemed to be their parents, but I'm sure someone had brought them and was responsible for them.

When the service was over, I spoke to the immediate family and then turned to the children. The woman would have been too old to be their grandmother, so I asked if she was their great-grandmother. "No," the girl said, "She is our friend." "What a lucky lady," I said, "to have two friends like you."

Something wonderful went on between those three, the older woman and the two small children. I expect it started with the woman. She reached out to them, and they responded. Somehow their relationship was strong enough for death, because the children were not frightened or distraught. Love is like that: It "bears all things, believes all things, hopes all things, and endures all things. Love never ends. . ." (1 Corinthians 13: 7-8).

# *Seeking God's Word to Me*

Whenever anyone tells me that there's only one way to read and interpret the Bible, I agree. Then quickly I say, "Yes, there's only one way, my way!" That, of course, is not the expected answer, because the speaker already has a fixed opinion about the Bible and is seeking either agreement or an opportunity to propagate that opinion.

I honestly believe there is only one way for me to read the Bible, and I cannot read it any other way. When I open its pages, I can only see it through my own eyes and my own understanding. What I "see" and what I "understand" have been greatly conditioned by who I am, what I've learned along the way, and what my deepest needs are at the time.

Let me give you an example. When I first began to read the Bible, with little or no understanding of it, I stumbled on a verse, 2 Timothy 1: 7, that said, "For God hath not given us the spirit of fear; but of power, and of love, and of a sound mind" (King James Version). Those words came to me like a gift from God, and they were.

At that time, they spoke to me about fear, "For God hath not given us the spirit of fear." Later those same words spoke to me about "power," "love," a "sound mind." The meaning of the verse or the emphasis on one of those words will change from time to time because my need was different, and God was speaking to my need.

Do you see what I'm driving at? If I am to follow the directions of the person who has "one way," then I must give over the Bible to be read through another's eyes and experience and accept God's word to another as God's word to me. In the end, I put more faith in the other person than I have in God's desire to speak to me through the pages of the scripture.

Various interpretations of the Bible are important, and no serious reader should disregard them. In the end, however, I believe the spirit of God is our guide as we read the Bible, and God brings its truth to us according to our need. In this sense, the process of reading and understanding the Bible has a personal element in it that can't be disregarded in favor of someone else's "one way" theory. To abandon that personal element is to give up one of the avenues that God has of speaking to us.

# *What's in a Name?*

I wrote myself a note the other day saying, "The spiritual world has no name."

That thought came after talking with a young man who had found, and was found by, God. He had a genuine awareness of a spiritual presence and realm that made his life full and whole. I might add that the experience was neither straight nor unusual. It was like arriving home after being away; it felt right, good, and as though everything was in its proper place.

The idea that "the spiritual world has no name" came to me because this man had no formal religious background or training. He didn't know too much about Methodists and Baptists, New Testament and Old Testament, incarnation and justification, etc.

Now, as one who came somewhere along the same road, I can tell you it helps to have a religious background, but it isn't absolutely necessary. God will open the door to those who are seeking God because God is seeking them.

God's kingdom is a reality! Whatever name we use does not alter or control it. The kingdom is discoverable by whatever name we have if we want to be a part of it.

There's a lake at home that's been there a long time. I'm sure the Indians named it and then settlers gave it another. As a boy, I knew it as Lake Butler; now it's called Lake Tarpon. (I still call it Lake Butler because I never fished or swam in anything called Lake Tarpon.)

In spite of the various names, it is the same body of water in the same location, and it was there before anyone named or renamed it. That, I think, is the way it is with God and the kingdom of God. It is there, it is real, and it can be experienced. It doesn't need a name to be or to be found.

# Thank You

What kind of person is it who can't say, "Thank you?" It might be a person so self-absorbed in a negative way that she couldn't see that something could have been done for her. On the other hand, it could be someone so painfully shy he was afraid to step out of his discomfort and say, "Thank you for what you have done for me." (I believe "Thank you" is the short form of this longer statement.) Perhaps some people become so egotistical they feel they deserve all the extra attention they get.

Enough analysis. How may such a condition be cured? The negative person could begin by learning that a lot of people enjoy doing nice things for others simply to show their affection. The shy person might discover that most other people are shy, too, and almost no one gets mad when you say thank you to them. The egotist might be a bit harder, but if everyone stepped back and did nothing for them, they'd soon discover there was no food on the table, clothes to wear, money for their needs, medicine for their ills, etc. They will quickly see how totally dependent they are on hundreds of silent people who play a part in their welfare.

The truth is that our lives are so blessed and sustained by the gifts of others that we simply could not survive without them. And that says nothing of the gifts of pure grace that come from those who love us.

What about God? Is God not obliged to give to us? No, but God does! Grace is the great word of the Bible—the free, unturned, unmerited love of God. There is more of it around than we ever imagined, both from God and from the people who care for us. The trick to discovering grace is to say "Thank you" whenever you see anything that looks like it. You'll be amazed at what happens to you and to whoever hears you say it.

# *Believing Too Little*

P. T. Barnum is often quoted as saying there is a sucker born every minute. But he also said that more people are fooled into believing too little than too much. I wonder if that isn't why some of us don't enjoy our life and faith as much as we could. We believe too little instead of too much.

Do you believe in yourself? How much do you believe in yourself? Do you believe in other people? How much do you believe in other people? Do you believe in God? How much do you believe in God?

What we call "the gospel," which simply means "good news," was given to us at Easter. The "good news" is that God has broken the power of evil over human life, has offered love and forgiveness to anyone who wants it, has triumphed over death and left a loving spirit in the world.

Now there's something to believe! More than that, something to live for. Believe as much of it as you can, and you'll find a great difference in your life and faith.

# Handling Disappointment

Whatever happened to Justus? He's the man who lost the election to become the twelfth disciple. Matthias and Justus were nominated to replace Judas. Matthias was chosen (Acts 1:21-26). Was Justus hurt, or did he accept it gracefully? The scripture doesn't say, only that the other man was the choice.

I am sure Justus was disappointed. He was a follower of Jesus from the beginning. Surely to become one of the twelve would be an honor beyond measure, yet he was passed by.

What we do with our disappointments may be more important than how we handle success. We usually measure up to success, but can we measure up to failure, especially when our self-esteem is at stake? If we do, we are able to overcome an egotism that always has to win or be first or succeed.

Realistically, no one can be a success all the time. To lose to another person can teach us, if we will let it, to rejoice in another's gain even if it is our loss. If it was desirable for us, it must be for them as well. Therefore, this disappointment for ourself can become joy for another when turned around.

Finally, and this happens frequently, failure can be an open door to a new venture that brings as much or more than we thought had been lost. Many a successful man or woman has had a serious failure some time.

And what about Justus? I have a feeling he went on to some significant service that brought joy to the Lord and himself. Why? Because he followed a Christ who didn't want him to fail and found a task equal to his ability.

# A Helping Hand

A young woman drove into the service station with a flat tire. The car was old and battered, and the other three tires weren't too far behind the first. I made some comment to Roy that there wasn't much point in putting on one tire because the others would blow out before she got much further down the street.

"Yeah," he said, "but these young kids don't have much money; they get by the best they can."

"What are you going to do?" I asked. "I've got a bunch of old tires out back. I'll give her one of those. If she comes back to pay me, it's O.K., and if she don't, it's O.K."

I left the station thinking that it's people like Roy who help you believe the world is all right and that there are a lot of good people left in it yet.

It doesn't take much to do what he did—a little time and energy, sharing something you have and the other person needs—but what a difference it makes. Not only does it provide a helping hand, but it shapes our attitude toward the world and other people.

It was this kind of thing our Lord loved to see and encouraged us to do. In fact, he prized such deeds so highly that he said, "Inasmuch as you have done it unto one of the least of these, you have done it unto me."

# *Mother Love*

I have a picture of my mother taken in the early nineteen forties. This particular portrait touches me deeply because it is the mother of my childhood and youth. Many of the memories of her center around those years of my life.

Not long ago we thought it was a good idea to have the picture reproduced and sent to her grandchildren as well as other members of the family. Taking it out of the frame, I found the following words written on the back:

> "This likeness of myself I had expressly made for my beloved husband, Porter, and my sons, Phillip and Eugene, equally beloved, all of whom I have failed in many ways, but nevertheless to whom I give my love and devotion. Keep always in remembrance of me."

> Marie Zimmerman
> April 1, 1942

When I could compose myself, I thought back to 1942. That was the year the war separated us as a family. Mom must have thought some of us might not see each other again. Fortunately, we did.

Then I read that part about being loved. I always knew that, never doubted it, and heard it said many, many times. As to failing us, she didn't. I had to live a while to realize that because she loved us so, she exceeded herself! I know now that she pushed past some of the problems and difficulties of her own life to give us more of herself than she believed she could or did.

Since we found her message, and as often as I think of it, I say, "Mom, you didn't fail us at all. You loved us each one, and we knew it; you gave us gifts of grace and beauty that we still have and remember." And then I say, "Lord, will you somehow get that message through to her?"

71

# *A Job Well Done*

I learned to use a cant hook one summer when I was seventeen and working in a saw mill. The man who taught me was the log turner. As the carriage returned from the saw, he would swing the cant pole behind him, bring it forward, and with a flick of his wrist open the hook, sink it into the wood, and with those powerful arms flip a giant log as though it was a coin. His motions were like a golfer with a classic swing or a baseball batter who moves in one, fluid motion. If I were watching, he'd look back, wink, and grin.

Some people would say it was a hard, menial job, somewhere near the bottom, but he turned it into a skill (which it is) and did it with a great artistry. He liked his work, did it well, and made it something for other people to see.

For some reason that I can't remember, I've always enjoyed watching a skilled person work: a typist, a carpenter, a cook, a lawyer. In all, there seem to be some of the same things the log turner had, pleasure in the task and pride in the work done.

Recently, I read that millions of people are unhappy in their jobs. I can understand that if working conditions are poor or the bosses irritable, but if it's the work itself, such misery is more a state of mind. I know. I learned to turn logs and liked it. Want me to show you how to swing a cant hook?

# *Quick and Easy*

The mail keeps bringing once-in-a-lifetime offers for sermon ideas and outlines that are quick, easy, and guaranteed to captivate the congregation. The latest (no joking) is Fifty-Two Easy to Present Devotions for Nearly Every Occasion. The thing that breaks my heart in receiving this information now is that it comes thirty years too late. Had it arrived when I started out, I could have coupled it with another publication that was popular in those days—Snappy Sermon Starters—and by now be a nationally known preacher.

There is no standard formula for preparing sermons. Each preacher has his or her own. But the best sermons don't come from the "here's how" manual; they are born out of something akin to Jacob's all-night wrestle with the angel. When it was over, Jacob limped away exhausted but exhilarated, saying, "I have seen God face to face, and yet my life is preserved" (Genesis 32:30).

It is only when the preacher has walked in the midst of life, wrestled with the biblical text, prayed, and studied that he or she is able to limp into the pulpit and proclaim the Word of the Lord. No less than that is required. When this is not done, you can tell very easily that the sermon is one of those Fifty-Two Easy to Present Devotions for Nearly Every Occasion.

# *Letting Go*

In more serious moments, I am much aware that nothing I have will be kept permanently. As a pastor, I have seen, at one time or another, the loss of those things we all value: homes, jobs, savings, health, family, and life itself. In truth, we hold nothing in permanent possession.

Though this is a somber thought, it isn't meant to be morbid, for the other side of that realization is that we can and do possess these things for a period of time and are richly blessed by them.

The awareness of such loss makes me ask, what then is permanent? What do I have that is mine forever? Of what can it be said, this will not be lost or taken away? My answer is: the promise of God to be with us always. That is one thing that the brevity and impermanence of life will not take away.

Jesus made a promise to his disciples that he would be with them always, even to the end of the world. That promise was not only to be present but to give strength and grace for life now and hope for the unknown future. When I find myself thinking of what I must give up for life now and hope for the unknown future or when I find myself thinking of what I must give up as life goes on, I take comfort and assurance in such a promise.

I have tasted God's grace in a difficult time and have had others tell me of it, too. Though I do not know how or when time will take me or my possessions, I strongly believe that God who is with me will provide in such a way that I shall see these temporary things replaced with something eternal. I believe also that this loss of earthly things will be understood then and far overshadowed by what God gives to take their place.

# *Laughter and Tears*

I saw it on the kitchen wall of a friend. It said, "Lord, teach me to laugh again, but please, dear God, don't let me forget that I cried." It struck me as one of those rare statements that is full of understanding and, in a few words, brings a message of hope.

Laughing and crying are as much a part of life as eating and sleeping. They are ways of expressing joy and sorrow, which we all experience. Because joy brings the delight and sorrow pain, we seek the one and try to seal ourselves off from the other. But the avoidance of suffering only delays joy and makes laughter hollow.

To accept suffering, one's own or another's, and to do so with faith and courage, brings us through feeling free and strong. It allows us to laugh again, not in a frivolous way, but from the deep-down discovery that nothing will separate us from the love of God and that we are never without God's help to restore us to strength and stability.

To stay in touch with laughter and tears is to be informed by each and imprisoned by neither. To laugh all the time is mockery; to cry continually leads to self-pity and destruction. When joy and sorrow inform each other and neither is forgotten, we find freedom and balance.

"In the world you have tribulation; but be of good cheer, I have overcome the world" (John 16:33).

# *The 'Get Ready' Man*

In *My Life and Hard Times*, James Thurber tells with great humor of interesting events in his family and home town. I like the story about the "get ready" man. Thurber said he "was a lank, unkempt gentleman with wild eyes and a deep voice who used to go about shouting at people through a megaphone to prepare for the end of the world. 'Get ready.' 'Get ready,' he would bellow. 'The world is coming to an end!'"

The "get ready" man and his kin have been around for a long time, so long, in fact, that his family tree can be traced back to the dawn of time. Somebody's always telling us the end is near. Of course, it will come some day, but I don't believe any time soon. (If it does, I shall apologize profusely for putting you at such ease that you were caught unaware.)

Why am I so confident about all this? Because I don't think God is through with the world yet. There's too much unfinished business to attend to. There are too many people on the edge of discovering what good things God has in store for us, too many people and places that haven't been won over yet.

Of course, this is where the "get ready" man steps in. He says things are so bad God is going to destroy it all. Well, that would mean God is giving up, and that I can't believe. Not if God "so loved the world that he gave his only begotten Son!" I say the creator's investment is too high and the results too great for God to quit now.

# *To Love and Honor*

One thing I have discovered about marriage is that most of us are strangers to each other when we marry and must spend a good bit of time getting to know and understand one another. Love is the glue that holds us together while this goes on.

Frankly, I don't think we ever get to know another person completely, but love allows us to accept him or her and, at times, to endure the person.

Also, since we never fully understand ourselves, how can we expect fully to understand someone else? At best, I think we even come to love the enigmatic nature of our partners, a nature that is sometimes strange even to them.

In the end, the mystery of another person's being is an interesting and exciting thing, and for someone to be willing to share it with you as best as he or she can is the most undeserved gift. Therefore, the thought of another person living with you and loving you enough to do that is very humbling and worthy of your love in return.

For me, that portion of the wedding ceremony that calls us to "honor" each other speaks to this need to love and to respect even when we do not understand.

# *Signs of the Christian*

A man once invited my wife and me to go to a neighboring town for a Sunday afternoon "hymn sing." On arriving, we found we were a week early and would have to come back next Sunday if we wanted to sing. However, as fortune would have it (good or bad, depending on how you look at it) another church was having a temperance meeting, and our host suggested we take it in, explaining that "One meeting is as good as another."

I've never subscribed to that philosophy about religious gatherings and did so even less that day. Although I believe in the cause, I sure didn't want to be caught in that crowd. It was one of those old-time, stomp-down temperance rallies where demon rum was denounced along with everybody who had anything to do with it.

I squirmed like a sinner at the judgment seat and would have walked out if we hadn't been there with someone else—and he having the time of his life. I didn't like the anger, the bigotry, the air of smug assurance. Pound for pound, there's more meanness in a religious bigot than most any other creature. Maybe it isn't meanness, but it's cold and unloving to the point of being cruel.

I attended a revival meeting one time in which the preacher breathed fire and fear on us and threats of what would happen if we didn't respond to his invitation. No one came forward except a frightened little girl who burst into uncontrollable tears. I had a terrible urge to go get her and leave the place and tell her on the way out how much God loves her and wanted the natural gaiety of her little-girl heart to be full of love.

It's obvious that a thing isn't religious just because it's held in a church and someone calls it Christian, but how do you discern? Jesus said of his disciples, "By their fruits you shall know them." Paul defined those fruits as love, joy, peace, patience, kindness, goodness, faithfulness, gentleness, and self-control. Whenever such a spirit is present, then we are justified in believing it is of God, and when it isn't, then I don't believe we are under obligation to call it God's.

# *Playing the Music*

I attended a concert one evening with a friend who is an accomplished musician. In fact, he played and taught the same instrument we had come to hear.

I enjoyed the evening very much, but without any training in music, I couldn't comment on the musician's mastery or technical ability. However, as we were leaving, someone in our party turned to my friend and asked, "Did he make any mistakes?" "He played beautifully and with great skill," my friend reply. "But did he make any mistakes?" the other person persisted. "Of course he made mistakes," he answered. "He played thousands of notes and was bound to make mistakes, but that's not what you listen for. It's how he presented and interpreted the music, and he did that beautifully."

It's not the mistakes you make but how you present and interpret the music! What a great way to look at life. Everybody makes mistakes; there's no way to avoid them. To act at all is to be open to error and mistake. But, if the desire and intent is to create some kind of music and we set out to do that for the joy of ourselves and the pleasures of others, then when the concert is over, the beauty of it will obscure the errors. Except, of course, for someone who likes to look for mistakes and find flaws in another person's performance.

I'm glad that God doesn't look for errors and count mistakes but listens for the music and knows the effort we put forth to play our individual instrument. There's hope and encouragement in that kind of audience.

# Half-hearted Days

I've been sitting and staring at this piece of paper for over an hour trying to think of something to write. I can't think of anything. At the moment, there's nothing that comes marching through my brain that must be said. Most of what's there seems dry and dusty. I suppose I could grind up something, but I'd be ashamed to admit it was mine. (Don't get me wrong; I produced some poor stuff, but at the time it was my best effort so I was willing to take credit for it.)

All I can think of at the moment is the literature of the saints that make mention of "dry times," periods when the spirit is still and communion with God seems to be broken. At such times, they brought these things before God as the best they could offer and prayed that it would burn more brightly on another day.

Do you suppose God will accept such gifts? When the dry times come can we say, "Lord, I have little to offer today. My spirit is dull, and I'm so caught up with the cares of the moment that I can't break away. Take this poor gift and by your grace put a luster upon it"?

Will God hear? I think so, for I believe God is willing to accept us at all times of life, at our best and at our worst. When we can't come whole-heartedly, then I think God is glad to see us come "half-heartedly," if that's the best we've got.

I've decided it isn't how much we've got to offer that counts but that we're willing to share with God whatever there is to give.

# Adequate Faith

I stumbled on a sentence in a book the other day that said in a few words what I firmly believe and think should be stated much more often than it is. Written by the Scottish theologian John Bailee, it said, "Faith always contains the idea of knowing and the idea of not knowing fully."

Most people believe their faith is inadequate. Deep down inside, they think there's so little faith it's hardly worth talking about, and secretly they suspect that others have found something they're still searching for.

I think this feeling clings to most of us because we grew up in an era when religion was thought of as something you "get," and, when you've "got" it, you know all, see all, hear all, and believe all. And yet, if we are to understand the New Testament, faith is not a possession or sudden disclosure; it is an allegiance. It is a confidence and trust that we place in God and in Christ who declared and revealed God to us.

When is our allegiance complete? When is our trust total? Can we ever say we have arrived? I doubt it. Paul said he hadn't. But people are not faceless because their faith is incomplete. Quite to the contrary, they may be people of great faith.

Rather than condemn ourselves and live with a sense of religious inadequacy, I think we ought to rejoice in what faith we do have and seek more. I've always liked that man who said to Jesus, "Lord, I believe; help my unbelief."

# *Becoming a Mature Person*

We were talking about what it takes to become a mature person, and she said, "You have to experience childbirth, the death of someone you love, and the need for forgiveness." The more I thought about the statement, the truer it became.

The first item I had to rearrange a bit, but I think it came out at the same place—being responsible for the care and guidance of another life from infancy to early adulthood. Child raising can teach you a lot of things you didn't know and correct some things you thought you did know. It requires an adaptability you never dreamed of having.

The death of a loved one is something we will all experience sooner or later. With the accompanying sorrow and separation, we are faced with the meaning of life and death in addition to the hurt we feel. How we accept such loss has much to do with how successfully we go on living. Grief can carry us into the deep places of the spirit where we meet God and find a richer understanding of life and death.

The need for forgiveness is something mature people realize about themselves after a while. To make a mistake and acknowledge it and to find that someone loves you enough to forgive it is to enter the holy of holies. It is to learn how love redeems. The realization of wrongdoing and the experience of forgiveness are so profound that we can never be the same person again.

For me, the heart of the Christian gospel is the love and forgiveness that God offers to those who realize their sins and mistakes. When this grace is truly felt, it has such life-changing effect that we are led from fragmentation to wholeness, from adolescence to maturity.

# *Exclaiming the Gospel*

I bought an old typewriter when I was in college that could be classified as an antique, but it worked well, and I beat out a lot of term papers on it. Due to age and long usage, it had some peculiarities about it, but because we were constant companions, I came to accept them as not out of the ordinary.

One of those oddities was the lack of an exclamation point. If you had to make one, you made it yourself by hitting two separate keys.

When you think about it, life doesn't supply the exclamation points either; we do. Life supplies the opportunities, and we give the exclamations. Hot dog! Yippee! Beautiful! Thank the Lord! These are exclamations that arise out of grateful hearts that can appreciate the many wonderful things that God in graciousness and people in their affection do for us. Christmas is one of the seasons that is full of exclamations, and I hope you'll spread yours around lavishly. Here are a few to choose from: Thank you! I love you! Christ is born! God is good! What a wonderful Church!

Pick out a couple of the above and make up some of your own. Add your exclamations to that of the angels who cried out, "Glory to God in the highest, and on earth, peace, goodwill towards all!"

# *High Noon*

We didn't get out of church until 12:15 the last time we took communion, but then the Lord's Supper always takes more time.

In the past, I felt anxious about such a service. The stress came because I was racing the clock, trying to get it all in before twelve. But one day a voice said, "Why?" "I don't know; it's supposed to be over by twelve." "Who said so?" "I don't know; it's just always been that way since I've been preaching." "Do you know what that says?" "No, what does it say?" "It says, 'O.K. God, you got an hour to do your thing. After that, we're leaving!'" "I don't know anybody who says that." "You don't have to; that's the way you act."

"Can't you see when your attention is on the clock you become more concerned with time than with God? Suppose God chose to make a move at 11:50 a.m. Would you, God's priest, say, 'You've got ten minutes to wrap it up?'" "No, of course not." "Well, you better not. God's liable to wrap you up."

"I've seen you cut the prayer, choose a short text, squeeze the meditation, and push people past the Lord's table. Why?" "To get out by 12:00 noon!" "Why?"

The conversation then came full circle again, and the voice wanted to know why we'd come in the first place, to be with God or to get out at noon.

I didn't know to whom I was talking. It may have been old Francis Asbury, that early American preacher who said, "How long were my services? An hour? Hardly! More closely four, and then two hours in prayer. Too long for you? Most likely. But I would argue that if your eyes are fixed on God and eternity, then six hours is no time at all. If they are fixed on the clock, then let the clock be your God, for there are no clocks in eternity."

God, if you'll spare us Brother Francis, we'll be glad to add an extra ten or fifteen minutes now and then.

# Great Bargains

I picked up a copy of People magazine one day and read an interview with a popular author. Among the several things she said about herself was, "I'm a practicing nothing. I have a strong rapport with the Lord. When I run out of money, when I'm scared, when a plane is landing, or when something is wrong with one of my children, then I make great bargains. 'Get me out of this one, sweet Jesus, and I'll never pull it again.'"

That's a pretty good description of how a lot of us relate to God, and I, for one, can't cast a stone because it's all too familiar. Only I used to say, "Get me out of this one, Lord, and I'll never cause you any more trouble." Then I'd cause more trouble.

Somewhere along the way, I began to wonder how I'd feel if the people I loved came to see me only when they wanted something. It wouldn't be long before I'd decide they weren't interested in me, only in what I could do for them. And after a while I'd feel used.

The God I believe in loves all of us and is glad to have us come for whatever reason, but how much more God must rejoice when we come seeking only the blessing of God's presence.

I'm not sure a person can be a "practicing nothing" and expect God to come every time he or she calls. It might be that one day God would get tired of being used and not answer. I want to be a "practicing something," not just to keep my accounts in good shape, but so that I may know and respond to the kind of God in John 3:16, who "so loved the world that he gave his only son."

# *Without Reproaching*

Lately, I've come upon two statements that focus on an attitude that is far too prevalent in our society and in the church as well.

The first statement is, "Blame is a sleazy theology concept" (*An Offering of Uncles*, Robert Capron). The second is, "If anyone lacks wisdom, let him ask God who gives to all men and without reproach. . ." (James 1:50). The King James Version uses the word "upbraiding" rather than "reproaching." It means severely critical, censorius.

"Blame" and "reproach" don't belong in the vocabulary of Christians because we live by Grace—that free, unmerited love of God that forgives and accepts sinners and struggles to help them overcome the sins that so easily beset them

I said the above two statements focus on a prevailing attitude among us. I see it all too often. It is evident in family life where we're constantly pointing out to each other, especially to children, what is wrong. It becomes such a way of life in many families that every member, child and adult, inwardly feels, "I can't ever do anything right." I've heard that said many times.

Then there's the church. It appears there, too. I've seen a carping, negative attitude almost envelope a church until everyone there began to feel on guard and defensive.

The insidious thing about "blame" and "reproach" is that those of us who have this attitude aren't aware of how seriously we are infected with it or how damaging it is to others. It's a disease that hides and masks itself to the afflicted.

What a wonderful opportunity Jesus had to "upbraid" and "blame" disciples after the resurrection. They had betrayed, denied, and fled from him, but he gathered them up, forgave them, and empowered them to become giants of courage and faith. That's what love and forgiveness will do for sinners. "Blame" and "reproach" only fix them more firmly in their sins and failures.

Thank you, dear God, for seeing the best in us and calling us forth to be that person until we can see and be a whole child of yours. Thank you, also, for not saying, "You've done it again!" and "Why do you always do that?" and "You're bad." Thank you for helping me to "make it" through the grace given in Jesus Christ. Amen.

# *Putting off Prayer*

I confess I often put off praying until I can no longer manage alone. I then begin to pray with feelings of guilt because I have waited until I needed something from God. Consequently, I start with an apology.

I found that I have never felt scolded when waiting so long, nor did God hold back from me because I withheld myself from God. It seemed God was glad I came and made me welcome. I admit I have not received instant answers to prayer. The answers came as I began to do something about the things for which I prayed. As the answers came, they felt like God's answers.

I declare when I stopped thinking of prayer as a way of getting God to do something for me and realized it was a place where we met in loving friendship, prayer became a whole new, joyous, wonderful thing.

I testified that I know God is real because prayer brings me into God's presence. (I do not experience a person so much as a Presence.) In that Presence, I know myself as a person whom God loves. In that Presence, too, I find a clearer, larger view of life that puts me on a higher plane than the scattered thoughts, fears, and anxieties that force me to pray.

I admit that, having used them, I know most of the reasons people don't pray, and if they would be laid aside to pray—in whatever word or way we choose—we would find a loving welcome and a personal word from God that was given for us.

# *Answering the Bell*

One of the routine things the Navy required in boot camp was to engage in some sport every Saturday morning. One Saturday, I was sent off to the gym to wrestle. I went with some apprehension, which moved up to panic when I walked in the gym and saw a Charles Atlas type flexing his muscles. (I don't mean the skinny guy who had the sand kicked in his face; it was Charles Atlas himself!)

The procedure was to give the referee your name and weight and he paired you with someone your size. Just to be sure I didn't draw "Atlas," I shaved five pounds off my weight.

Finally, my name was called, and as I climbed over the ropes, to my horror, Atlas was coming over the other side! My first thought was of instant death; my second, that he lied about his weight.

With all that talk about being fighting men and never disgracing the Navy and the flag, there was no backing out. Standing alone and friendless in my corner, I decided to rush out and leap on my opponent to get in the first lick before being mangled and carried off to the sick bay. At least there would be some honor in the effort, and I wouldn't be called "chicken" for that, even though I expected to look like a fresh-picked one right after the fight.

The bell rang, and I leaped straight at him! Down we went, I on top and he on bottom. I held his shoulders tight to the mat and heard the referee start to count. Atlas squirmed, but he was no match for me. "This guy's weak," I thought. "He can't get up!" The match didn't last more than thirty seconds.

Climbing down from the ring, I was trying to understand what happened. I overestimated his strength; I underestimated mine; I have forgotten what do or die determination can accomplish.

There are a lot of struggles in life, and we probably won't win them all, but we will surely win more often if we jump on them with "last chance" determination. With that, you can even make Charles Atlas come tumbling down now and then.

# 'I Belong Here'

The service was over, and we were in the social hall getting better acquainted. I had come to preach a series of sermons and welcomed the opportunity to meet some of the people personally. I spoke to an elderly woman and introduced myself. She replied by telling me her name and saying, "I belong here."

At first, I didn't understand what she meant but then remembered there were people present from other churches. She was saying, "I am a member of this church." That's what the words said on the surface, but there was a depth to them that meant much more. I began to understand this as I saw her at every service and at the Bible study.

She "belonged" to that church in the sense that it was her church and she had a place there. It was her church in the same way that her home was hers. This is the place I love, and this is where I live. I belong here.

To be able to say "I belong here" is to say a lot about yourself, where you are, and who you are.

I want to say that about the world—"I belong here"—and revel in the joy of my own life and in this fascinating place. I want to have the feeling of belonging with my family and friends, the city where I live, the house I live in, the church I serve.

Deep down, I want to know that I belong to God. Wherever God is and wherever God's work goes on, I want to say, "I belong here," and feel it deeply.

We have a sense of belonging wherever our hearts are at home. What a wonderful thing for someone to say about the church.

# *Mysteries of the Spirit*

I am reading *Report to Greco* for about the third time now. I will pick it up again in two or three years and find still more things that were missed in previous readings. The book is the spiritual autobiography of Nickos Kazantzakis, author of *Zorba the Greek*, St. Francis, *The Last Temptation of Christ*, and several others.

It was the lifelong work of Kazantzakis to probe the mystery of the spirit, both human and divine. Even as a child, his searching mind was always looking behind and underneath human attitudes and actions. In the beginning of the Report, as he tells of his childhood in Crete, Kazantzakis says, "These two, birth and death, were the very first mysteries to throw my childish soul into ferment. I kept beating my tender fist against this pair of closed doors to make them open. I saw that I could expect help from nobody. Everyone either remained silent or laughed at me. Whatever I was to learn I would have to learn by myself."

What a tragedy that people either left or remained silent when a young boy asked about life and death, and he was left on his own to find out what he could. What would you say if a child asked, "How was I born and why?" "What is it like to die, and what happens after that?"

Of course, these things are mysterious to us, but we know something about them, and our faith tells us more. I'm speaking more openly about birth and death and what we believe about it. There's much in the Bible concerning both. We could start with the words of the first woman who had the first baby: "I have gotten a man with the help of the Lord" (Genesis 4:1) and then go to those of Jesus: "I am the resurrection and the life; he who believes in me, though he died, yet shall he live, and whoever lives and believes in me shall never die" (John 11:25-26).

# Recruiting Disciples

He was my mentor, Thaxton Springfield. He stood at a critical conjunction of time and place when I was trying to find myself and my life's work. He said he was recruiting ball players for the Methodist Student House, but he wasn't; he was recruiting people to become disciples of Christ.

I joined the team, dropped by the student house, helped out here and there, was given a free room in return for janitorial work, was asked to assist in the Sunday services, was called on to speak at a small country church, and wound up in the ministry—all the while exposed to endless hours of Thaxton's love, laughter, and conversation. He said he never wanted to influence me to go into the ministry. I believed him then. I don't now.

Shortly before he died, his friends collected some of his sermons and put them in a book. I couldn't read them then; it was too close and too personal. I'm reading them now, one each morning as a devotion to him as well as to my God and his, the God he helped me know so much better.

Many of the characteristic words and ideas of these sermons revive dormant memories and experiences, some with deep emotion, and I am reminded all over again of the limitless time and affection he gave me. The biblical word for this is incarnation: the spirit of God in the body of a human being.

It was the way of Jesus, who was a full and perfect example of incarnation. It was the way of Thaxton Springfield, and, because it was, there are many more like me who believe and follow the Incarnate Christ. I must pass it on. It is the only proper way to repay the man who shared the spirit of God so freely with me.

# Asking for Proof

People were often asking Jesus for "signs," some concrete evidence that he was the Christ, God's Son. It was a way of asking him to offer proof of himself so they could be certain.

When you look closely at a request like that, you begin to see the first concern was to be certain, to be reassured, to have knowledge of him before they accepted him.

I liken that to a romantic relationship in which a young man or woman says to the other, "Prove your love to me. Do something that will make me believe beyond a shadow of a doubt that you love me more than anyone else and always will. Do this before I say yes to you."

If this kind of demand persists, then the one who is asked for the "sign" will realize the most important thing is not a loving relationship but the need for reassurance. And if that person is wise, he or she will know that the need for reassurance will continue and often be greater than the relationship itself.

So Jesus didn't offer a sign; he offered himself. He asked for faith, which is another word for trust, and faithfulness, another word for fidelity.

Only in faith and faithfulness do we ever come to know if love is genuine or Christ is the Son of God. Answers given before a relationship starts will never provide the assurance we want. We will "know" only after we have trusted Christ and followed him. Then we will know for ourselves and not have to ask anyone else, not even Jesus.

# *The Music of the Morning*

It was a beautiful morning. The air was fresh and crisp. Birds were singing, and squirrels were jumping from limb to limb and skittering around the tree trunks. It was a perfect time for a walk, I thought, as I went out for the morning paper.

On reaching the edge of the driveway, I saw a man out for a stroll, but there was something unusual about him; he had an antenna on his head. Yes, sticking up over his head was a six-inch antenna, and clapped to his ears were two radios. I watched in amazement. When the world was waking up and there was so much to hear of its stirring sounds, he was drilling his brain with the radio. The music of the morning was being played for him all through the trees and shrubs, and he was passing it up for the top 40 or the traffic report.

I, for one, am grateful for radio and television. I enjoy them both in their place, but I am increasingly concerned that we are becoming a nation of passive watchers and listeners—letting someone else tell us what to see and hear and how to feel about it.

Watching television can become an addiction and leaving the radio on a habit. In fact, some people feel uncomfortable without background music or something to see. To surround yourself with programmed sights and sounds is to miss seeing and hearing many beautiful things that are going on in the natural world. I'm making a plea to turn it off now and then and go outside to see and hear the real thing for yourself.

I'm thinking about asking the government to set aside a ten-mile square in the middle of a big national park and prohibit any mechanical thing inside it. No cars, trucks, bicycles, radios, televisions, saws, hammers, axes, etc., only what nature has placed there. At the entrance, I would put a large sign that said, "Come inside and see, hear, taste, and touch the world in its original state!"

I have a feeling that our hungry souls would feast on the sights and sounds and smells. It would fill a void that we've forgotten because of the manufactured sounds that have occupied that space.

If you want to get started before I persuade the government to set up the ten-mile square, take a walk some early morning and leave off the earphones.

# *Word Power*

The advertising flyer billed it as the "Christian event of the year." A popular music group was coming to town, and, according to the pitch, the appearance would eclipse any religious event that had or would happen this year. What bothered me about this was the use of exaggerated language to the point of untruth in an effort to sell tickets and pack the house.

I don't have any problems with advertising or advertising religious events. It's the abuse of language in the distortion of truth, of which this flyer was a gross example, that I object to.

Take exaggerated language, for example. We've heard "fantastic," "terrific," "absolutely," "marvelous," etc., until they don't mean anything. I contend that if you use up such words praising cat food or corn flakes, then you don't have any left to describe the birth of a baby or a new romance. Also, you lose the ability to distinguish between the mundane and the important because such words are used indiscriminately.

The distortion of truth is even worse. It becomes misleading and deceptive and, in the end, dishonest. To say that the appearance of a musical group is the most important Christian event of the year is not only untrue, it's an offense to the truth.

The most important Christian event of the year will more likely have something to do with the number of people who are hoping and praying, "Thy kingdom come, thy will be done on earth as it is in heaven." When that happens, jump up and shout at the top of your voice, "marvelous," "fantastic," "wonderful," "nothing like it in the whole world," "free," "absolutely free," "come one, come all."

Save up some of the best and biggest words in your vocabulary and bring them to church next Sunday. Use them to praise God for what God is doing with us and our world and employ them to convince other people to join with us.

# Saint and Sinner

Browsing through a library one day, I came upon the collected writings of Robert Louis Stevenson. Oftentimes, among the works of a great writer, are collected letters, articles, and short stories that aren't as familiar as the more celebrated work. There was such a book, and in it I read the most devastating attack on gossip I have ever seen. It was an open letter to the Rev. Dr. Hyde of Honolulu about Father Damien.

Father Damien, you will remember, was the Belgian priest who chose to live and work in the leper colony at Molokai. Eventually, he contracted leprosy as a result of living and serving there. What prompted Stevenson's letter was another letter that had been published by a minister who said that Damien was a coarse, dirty man, headstrong and bigoted, and the leprosy of which he died should be attributed to his vices and carelessness.

Stevenson went to Molokai to learn more about Damien (who was then dead) and what he had done there. He found that some of the things said of the priest were true, though he heard nothing about immorality. What he discovered was that Father Damien had flaws in his character; he was coarse, headstrong, and dirty. Yet, at the same time, he had a great heart and sacrificed himself in God's service to the lepers. Side by side was greatness and smallness in the same man.

But isn't that true of all of us? Have we not all sinned and fallen short of the glory of God? Nowhere on earth is there a pure saint or a perfect sinner; there are only people whose wills move them towards one or the other condition and whose lives often reveal both.

Stevenson wrote to the Rev. Dr. Hyde: ". . . I take it . . . that you are one of those who have an eye for faults and failures; that you take a pleasure to find and publish them; and that having found them, you make haste to forget the overvailing virtues and the real success. . . ."

If God, who knows our faults, canceled our limited success because of them, who can stand before God? The good news is that God forgives our sins and nurtures the goodness and virtue found within us. Can we do less for each other?

"Father, forgive us our trespasses as we forgive those who trespass against us."

# Computer Correspondents

I'm not at all impressed that a computer knows my name and address and writes me letters. The fact is that several computers know and write me. Usually, they say something like, "We have chosen you especially MR. GENE ZIMMERMAN OF 909 GRANADA BLVD. because you are among that select group of people who appreciate fine things. When you receive your lovely hand-crafted orangutan covered in simulated pearls, you will recognize immediately that is worth much more than the $4.98 you will pay for the postage charges."

Lately, I thought about answering some of those warm, flattering letters by saying something like this: "Dear COMPUTER NO. 739654-Z2 high atop the Apex Building in downtown Chicago: I am writing to you at 1934 GRAND AVE. to tell you, with some embarrassment, that I had forgotten we were such fast friends or that you remembered my interest in pearl-handled monkeys. As to the monkey, I have enough now and, if you send me yours, will regretfully have to send it back unclaimed. Fondest regards to all my old friends there in the Apex Building."

What does impress me is when some human friend takes time to write because he or she is thinking of me and remembers where I live.

Most of all, I'm impressed that God knows who and where I am with all of my life with interest and affection.

My vital statistics kept in a computer and sent to me in a mechanical letter don't impress me at all. Those that are kept in the heart of God impress me more than I can say.

# Learning the Right Notes

I was listening to a recording recently in which there was a beautiful trumpet solo. Though I'm not a qualified critic, it sounded flawless to me and so smooth as to seem effortless. It was, of course, the offering of a skilled musician, and only he would know the countless hours of hard work that lay behind that skilled presentation.

Funny how your mind works sometimes. After the music ended, I wondered how many sour notes he blew before he could play so well. With that in mind, I began to visualize a little boy at home blasting away on his farm with the whole family relieved when the session was over. Then I saw the music teacher, who knew how the instrument ought to be played, going over and over the same lesson until it was finally learned.

Patience! That's what it takes, patience! Patience on the part of a child who wants to play an instrument; patience on the part of those who teach; patience on the part of those who have to listen and wait for that great day when the notes are all put together properly.

Thank God for those people who are patient with us, not just about music lessons, but life in general. No one picks up the instrument of life to make sweet music without practice, instruction, encouragement, endurance, and patience.

Right now, I'm grateful for my parents and a host of people whose loving patience could wait for me to find the right notes. Most of all, I'm grateful for a loving God whose patient love seems to have no end. Surely God's choice must be boundless when you finally get it right and come play for God's pleasure as well as our own.

# A Family Reunion

I read a magazine article one day about a young man who went to Ireland to visit the area where his grandfather had come from. His American family was quite small—the mother and father, an aunt, and himself—and he wanted to find his "roots." The aunt remembered the names of one or two relatives, and, with these in hand, he went to Ireland.

What he found was overwhelming. He was greeted like a long-lost son, not by one person, but dozens. Some of the older ones remembered his grandfather so took him from house to house to introduce him to his kinfolk. "After a day of visiting relatives," he said, "it was impossible to eat or drink another thing, especially tea."

My eyes moistened when I read the end of the article. The author, Timothy O'Keefe, said, "I was preparing to leave when Pat took me to the highest point on this farm and said, 'Look around you, Tim, in all directions, at the many farms you see. You may have a few people in America, but, as far as you can see, everyone is related to you in one way or another. You have a home here.'"

That's exactly what we ought to tell people when they come to church! "Look around you . . . as far as you can see, everyone is related to you in one way or another. You have a home here." And our warmth and welcome should be proof of it.

The church, for me, is the family of faith. It is made up of people who know God as parent, Christ as Lord, and each other as brothers and sisters in the "household of faith," to use Paul's phrase. And when folks enter the church, we should make them welcome in such a way that they feel as though they have arrived in time for the family reunion. And when they leave, they should know they have a home here.

# *Discovering What's Important*

There was a news article in the paper recently about a man whose wife and two children had been adrift in a boat for three days. The family had been fishing in the Cayman Islands when their motor ran out of gas. Since they were close to shore, the father swam in for help, but the boat drifted away. Three days later, they were found 40 miles from the island.

It was what the father said that caught my attention: "I now know what's important and what isn't." This he said in response to finding his family and in expressing his gratitude for all the people who helped him.

To be able to say, "I know now what is important and what isn't" is to come to one of the most significant places in life. It is to know the things that have the greatest meaning and value for you. I honestly believe that most of us start out looking for such things but struggle or discouragement makes us give up and settle into a self-centered existence.

At this point, you're probably thinking that I'm going to get "religious" in the next line or two. Yes and no. No, in the sense that one does not have to be narrowly religious to realize that the love of family, the need for friends (and being one), and the enjoyment of the natural world are among the highest values. Yes, in the sense that these are among those things that the Christian faith places at the center of its interest, believing that God has given them to enrich and ennoble our common life.

Discovering what's important and what isn't is, to a large extent, a lifelong pursuit. We put it together as we go along. Catastrophe will often clarify it for us, but that's the hard way. How much better to be looking for the best as you go and embracing and enfolding each thing as you discover it.

It is the business of the church to help people find and live with those most important things. To do so is to discover life's greatest meaning and highest joy.

I believe we will have "arrived" when we can say, as did the man in the Cayman Islands, "I now know what is important and what isn't."

Lifting the Dark Cloud

Today began as a gloomy day for me. I would have preferred to disappear for a while, taking a long walk somewhere or spending the day alone in a boat. Since that couldn't be, I came on to work feeling a bit like the character in "Lil' Abner" who walked around with a dark cloud over his head. Fortunately, the gloom didn't last too long because two or three people passed by and, without their knowing it, renewed my spirit.

I am deeply grateful for people whose cheerful affection renews and restores our sagging spirits. The Apostle Paul particularly appreciated such folk and thanked them by name: "I rejoice at the coming of Stephanas and Fortunatus and Achaicus . . .for they refreshed my spirit . . ." (1Corinthians 16:17-18). "May the Lord grant mercy to the household of Onesiphorus, for he often refreshed me. . ." (2 Timothy 1: 16). And to Philemon, he said, "I have derived much joy and comfort from your love, my brother, because the hearts of the saints have been refreshed through you" (Philemon 1: 7).

Such is our calling as Christians, to refresh the hearts of others, though now and then we also need it ourselves. Today, I want to say, "I derived much joy and comfort from your love, Emily Ann, Tom, Charles, and Connie."

# A Definition of Faith

Isn't it nice to hear the preacher say something you already believe? There is a comfort in it that confirms what you think, so you can sit there and say to yourself, "Well, at least two of us are right."

One notch above that is to see it in print. That's what happened to me one day. I was reading along, and suddenly the writer was saying something I strongly believe. What was it? "We know somehow that to have faith is to be actively disposed to trust in and to be committed to someone or something. To have faith is to be related to someone or something in such a way that our heart is invested, our caring is committed, our hope is focused on the other" (Life Maps, Jim Fowler and Sam Keen).

That's the best definition of faith I know and the one I'll stand on. Faith is not a possession. It's not something you get. It is not something that hits you or happens to you. It isn't even proper doctrine. It's trust and commitment. It's relating to someone or something in such a way that your trust has a way of controlling and directing your life.

In the Christian meaning of the word, faith is trusting in and being committed to Christ. It can be said even more simply than that: "Only the person who decides that Jesus was right becomes a Christian and the decision is what coming to faith is all about" (*The Bible in the Pulpit*, Leander Keck).

To decide that Jesus is right! Right about God, right about people, right about life, and then living on the basis of that belief—that's faith!

In the light of that definition, it isn't so much what you see or what you feel but that you've come to the conclusion Jesus was right and you want to live your life on the basis of that belief. If you will follow that direction, knowledge and experience will come until, someday, you may be able to say with the Apostle Paul, "I know whom I have believed, and I am sure that he is able to guard. . .what has been entrusted to me" (2 Timothy 1:12).

# *Predicting the End of the World*

The end of the world came and went last week. I didn't inquire too much into it beforehand because I wasn't expecting it to happen.

Predicting the end of the world has been a pastime for centuries. In fact, I was reading just this morning about the disciples asking Jesus when it would happen. His answer: ". . .of that day and hour no one knows, not even the angels of heaven, nor the Son, but the Father only" (Matthew 24:36). Since God alone knows, don't check the paper to find out or read the latest weird book that has it predicted.

I don't worry about God ending the world; I worry sometimes that we will. I fear that out of some kind of national insanity, human beings will start hurling nuclear bombs at each other, and, when that stops, it won't look like the world.

But even in the face of our madness, I have faith that God has a divine purpose for our world. God has given too much to it and suffered too much for it to let foolish people take it out of divine control. How do I know that? From the cross and the resurrection! The cross is the price God has paid for the world; the resurrection is God's intention to succeed with it. Our responsibility is to work for God's intention and just stand against the madness.

# Solicitation

The morning was left free to prepare for the Good Friday service. Some unexpected things, all of them important, had taken so much time that I left the church and went home to avoid further interruption. What I had hoped to do at a leisurely pace had now become a demanding necessity.

The phone was ringing as I walked in the door. Since our son was in the hospital, I must answer. The voice said, "Reverend Zimmerman, this is Sandy. I'm from Ajax Products. Can I have a minute of your time?"

Disguising my dislike for telephone solicitations, I said, as nicely as possible, "No, Sandy, I can't give you a minute of my time today. In less than an hour, I'm speaking at a worship service, and I must be ready for it."

"Then may I have just a moment?" she asked. (What persistence, what brass!)

"Sandy, I don't even have one moment I can give you." She replied, "I was going to ask if you would pray for me. I have emotional problems, and I need your help. What you are doing today is more important than my trying to sell you something."

I said, "Sandy, I will give you more than a moment of my time. I am going to the study now, and the first thing I shall do is pray for you. God loves you very much, and even though we have never met, I love you, too. Thank you for calling me."

Before the Good Friday meditation began, I prayed for Sandy. Her request brought us before the crucified Christ whose outstretched arms were open to her, to me, and the whole world. Surely today, of all days, Christ would hear the cry of someone who was suffering. When the prayer was finished, the meditation began without moving from the place or the purpose of the prayer.

"Lord, did you do that on purpose to prepare me for Good Friday, or did it just happen that way?"

# *Testing the Spirits*

I'm of the opinion that anyone with a strong faith needs a healthy dose of skepticism to go with it. The reason is that, in the realm of religion, we hear things that go from strange to weird and from weird to crazy.

In the name of God, we've witnessed mass suicide with the followers of Jim Jones and what appears to be mass hypnosis. The tragedy is that too many people are willing to turn themselves over to anyone who will provide ultimate answers.

The Bible cautions us about being too quick to believe. Jesus warned his disciples to "Take heed that no one leads you astray. Many will come in my name. . ." (Mark 13:5-6). Ephesians admonishes us not to be "tossed to and fro and carried about with every wind of doctrine, by the cunning of men. . ." (Ephesians 4:14), and John says, "Beloved, do not believe every spirit, but test the spirits to see whether they are of God; for many false prophets have gone out into the world" (1 John 4:1). His tests were that the Christ had come to us "in the flesh" (as a human being) and that love is the standard for Christian life in judgment: ". . .he who loves is born of God and knows God. He who does not love does not know God; for God is love" (1 John 4:7-8).

Recently someone asked how, in the face of all the religious stuff we hear, can one know what is true. My quick reply was, "Keep one foot on the floor." Realizing that remark may have revealed some misspent youth, I went on to say, "Use your common sense."

I'm convinced that God communicates with us through the reasonableness of our own judgment and we can trust it. The other alternative is to lay our judgment aside and take at full value what anyone tells you, and I'm not ready to do that.

Here are some guides for dealing with the uncertain questions of faith. Is it scriptural? Where does it stand in the long history of Christian tradition? Is it reasonable? What does your experience tell you? That's not a bad way to "test the spirits."

# A Model of Christian Diplomacy

One of the letters of Paul that is seldom read or used for sermons is the letter to Philemon. I chose it the other day as a devotion and was so blessed by it I want you to read it too. It's so brief it can be read in a minute or two.

Apparently Philemon became a Christian under Paul's ministry (vs. 19) and Paul a welcome guest in his home (vs. 22). Philemon had a slave Onesimus who also became a Christian, and, when he heard Paul was in prison, he ran away to be with him and serve him (vs. 10).

The letter has to do with the return of Onesimus to his master and is a model of Christian diplomacy. It reveals a deep affection from both men. It calls each to accept the other as a Christian brother. It lays a gentle but firm restraint on Philemon not to abuse Onesimus.

Paul said, ". . .I am bold enough in Christ to command you to do what is required, yet for love's sake I prefer to appeal to you" (vs. 8).

"I prefer to do nothing without your consent in order that your goodness might not be by compulsion but of your own free will" (vs. 14).

". . .If you consider me your partner, receive him as you would receive me. If he has wronged you at all, or owes you anything, charge that to my account" (vs. 17-18).

". . .I wrote to you, knowing that you will do even more than I say" (vs. 21).

I was moved by several things in this short letter but most by the loving way that Paul dealt with a potentially explosive problem that could have left both men less than Christian. I finished with the hope that I, too, could fix my own conflicts and disagreements in the same spirit.

One of the bishops of the early church was named Onesimus. If he is the same person in Paul's letter (and I like to think he is), then the message found its mark. Responding with Christian love and diplomacy does work and bears much fruit.

# In Love and War

How often have you heard, "All's fair in love and war?" Many times, I'm sure. Have you thought about what it says when looked at seriously? A song on the radio kept repeating it until something inside me said, "That's stupid—no, more than that—shocking, because love and war are at the opposite ends of the spectrum."

There's nothing to compare between love and war. In war, the other person is the enemy. In war, the purpose is to confuse and deceive the enemy, inflicting pain and loss until they concede superior strength and surrender.

How's love comparable to war? In truth, it isn't, but there is an increasingly visible dark side to that saying: the violence, the deception, and the domination of one person over another in marriage and families. Sometimes rules of war are applied to the very place where love reigns—our homes. The one place in the world where we ought to be safe from harm is at home; for some, it is not.

To love another as God loves us is at the heart of the Christian gospel. We who claim that faith should resolve daily to do just that, beginning with those nearest us and then reaching out to those farthest away. It is God's way with us.

# Worthwhile Lives

Occasionally, a pastor is called on to talk to someone who wants to take his own life. The pastor must try to convince him that life is worth living.

If you were called on to persuade someone that life was worthwhile, what would you say? That's not a catch question, and I'm not hiding over here in the corner with the answer. I ask it so we will examine ourselves to lay hold of those things that are most valuable and important to us, things that bring joy, excitement, and richness and make life worthwhile.

Name the people, places, and things that bless you. Thank God for them and look for ways to express your gratitude.

I have a strong feeling that if we examine why our lives are worth living and daily express our gratitude for these gifts (and they are gifts), we can help many people see, before they become desperate, that God-given life is very worthwhile.

# *The Monkey on Our Backs*

I don't like for people to put the monkey on my back. If you're familiar with the term, you're familiar with the experience. It's a common attempt to place the blame on you. Sometimes it's done blatantly and other times so subtly it's there before you are aware of it.

There are a number of ways to do it, so many, in fact, I won't mention the obvious ones, just some of the more subtle ones. For example: "Oh, I'm sorry; I thought you knew we wanted you to do that." Or, "That's all right; we'll call on someone who has more time." There are others, such as, "We missed you at the meeting." (You can tell by the tone of the voice whether you were missed or not.)

All of these can be innocent words, of course, but sometimes aren't. And when they aren't, it's easy to tell the difference.

It's the attitude I don't like—the attitude that you must pay for something someone thinks is wrong and they must get in a dig. Because I dislike this attitude so, I try hard not to exhibit it.

Some say we place blame because we feel guilty and try to rid ourselves of it by making others feel guilty. Maybe that's it. I don't know, but I do know this: God doesn't do it!

God doesn't goad and snipe and load us down with condemnation. God redeems us! God restores us! God forgives our sins, and God sets us free! Glory be and hallelujah: there is someone who will take the monkey off our backs!

# Fine Tuning

There were five of us at the table and an animated conversation. The restaurant was filled with many sounds of people talking, waiters removing dishes, and customers getting up and sitting down. Had you asked if there was any music to be heard, I would have said no. Suddenly, in the midst of it all, I heard the warm mellow notes of Paul Desmond's saxophone cut through that din of sounds.

You might think I'm some kind of musicologist to do a thing like that. I'm not. I just liked the Dave Brubeck quartet back in the 60s and, most of all, Paul Desmond's sax. He had a unique style, distinctively his own and still easy to identify.

What is surprising is that I heard no music until something I enjoyed and had trained myself to hear came through. The brain is a fascinating thing, isn't it? Without a conscious awareness of music, it quickly picked out of all that sound something I like and brought it to my attention.

This leads me to believe that your mind, sometimes on a subconscious level, is at work picking up on things that are important to you. If you like people, you'll keep meeting people to like; if you're looking for the good that abounds, you'll see it again and again. Are you looking for God in the things God is doing? Tune your mind to that, and you'll be surprised when, through the many sounds of life, some clear note comes that says, "I am the Lord thy God."

# *Prayer Meeting*

I stopped by Ellzey Methodist Church for prayer meeting one night. In case you'd liked to go sometime, Ellzey, Florida is two miles past Otter Creek on State Road 24 heading to Cedar Key. That's where I started preaching, and both the place and people are still dear to me.

As I went in, I saw a motor scooter parked outside loaded down with camping gear. Some camper, I thought, who saw the lights and stopped in. He was sitting on the back row, a man in his early fifties, looking more as if he camped in his clothes than under the tent. No one should appear to be out of place in church, but he did.

After the lesson was over, the pastor invited us to come forward for prayer. All ten of us went up, and I wondered how the other visitor would respond. He came too.

The prayers began. The preachers reeled theirs out with practiced ease; the children were slow and timid; one or two others spoke a bit awkwardly as though unaccustomed to praying out loud. Then it was the camper's turn. He began talking to Someone, not us.

He thanked God for the mystery of God's Presence, the joy of God's company. He offered praise that God's people, though diverse, were one in God. He prayed on, and the atmosphere of the church began to change. I felt that we were being gathered up and presented to Someone who is very real and very present.

When it was over, we met the man of prayer and learned a little about him, though not too much. He said he was on his way to Texas to spend some time in a monastery. "How did you happen to stop here?" I asked. He smiled and replied, "I'm looking for real things, and, whenever I find one, I stop to enjoy it."

I thought I understood what he meant, for that place and those people were real; that night, God was, too. The stranger made God real for us.

# *An Anonymous Letter*

I received an anonymous letter this week. Ministers get more than you might think, and, consequently, I've learned to spot them. One clue is no return address. The greeting is a tip off, too, such as, "Who do you think you are?" From there, it's usually downhill, falling into the category between "mean" and "nasty" and ending with an occasional threat about what God is going to do to "apostate preachers." Sometimes, there is an addendum that says, "I'm going to stop giving to the church if you don't stop. . . ."

I won't tarry to look for the reasons people send such letters. I'm sure you can think of some yourself. I'm writing about this one because it was different. I had braced myself for some critical remarks, but when the letter was opened, I was blessed by its message.

She was only asking for prayer. Believing that God loves us and will help us, she asked that I pray for a need that was not explained. Now I understood why it was unsigned. I did not have to know the name or the need; God knows both. I only needed to do what I was lovingly requested to do: pray. I did, and I will.

The dearest part of the letter was the way it was signed: "Your sister in Christ."

Dear sister in Christ:

> Forgive me if this letter in any way publicizes you or your request. That was the last thing I wish to do. It's just that I want you to know, in case you read this, that you have blessed my life with your faith. Also, I want to tell you that not only am I praying but I shall ask others to pray as you have requested. Thank you for signing the letter "Your sister." I've always wanted a sister.
>
> Sincerely, your brother,
> Gene Zimmerman

# The Risks of Loving

He was a bull of a man. His hands were twice as large as mine, and his arms were the size of my legs. A big chest pulled out at his shirt and left small gaps from button to button. Obviously, hard work had made this strong body. In the face of such strength, there was a gentleness that was unplanned and unnoticed by him.

He had come to ask if I would conduct a funeral service for his wife. It happened suddenly, he said. His back was turned when he heard a sound, and, turning around, he found her dead. As he described what had happened, a low moan begin to rise up out of that great chest. The strength of the man and the sound within his body made a noise like an ox about to bellow. He did his best to stifle the cry, but it forced its way out in a burst of grief. That strong body could not contain his anguish.

He said she was ill as a child and was told that she could not live long; when they married, she was warned not to have children but did anyway. The children are grown now, and she's dead, and her husband is grief-stricken.

I have not moved from the place where we sat. The room is heavy with grief. I can still hear the sound of his groaning. He left, that strong man, carrying his terrible burden with him.

I asked myself, "Was it worth it? Would you take such a risk if you knew it would come to this?" I could run down the hall and call him back to ask. There's still time but no need. I am certain he would stare at me as though I had lost my mind.

"Thank you, God, for a courageous woman who dared to live in the face of death, who risked her life to bear life, and whose love gave a strong man a great heart and gentle touch. Please, God, take care of him now that she is no longer here. Amen."

# *Doing Good*

I read a statement by Henry David Thoreau that made me laugh out loud. "If I knew for certain that a man was coming to my house with a conscious design of doing me good I would run for my life," he said.

I guess what he was talking about is a "do-gooder," a common phrase that is used these days. I take it to mean someone who is trying to get us to do something he or she thinks ought to be done. In that sense, many of us would run for our lives.

On the other hand, the person who would be more welcome is a "be-gooder." A be-gooder, in my judgment, is someone who wants to make your life richer just for your sake, not for theirs. This is the kind of person who is always bringing something good, saying something good, trying to share something good with us. In that sense, we would delight to see such a person come.

# Trial and Error

Just before Christmas, I spent some time in a woodwork shop making gifts for several people. The item I was making was one I'd seen. I thought it was simply made and could be easily reproduced. I tend to make judgments like that and as a result have discovered one of life's underlying rules: Few things are as simple as they seem or as easily reproduced.

As a result of the above-mentioned rule, I made several mistakes at the outset. Boards were cut too short; some holes were drilled in the wrong place. By the end of the day, however, I had learned through both mistakes and success and was pleased with the outcome.

Some time during that day, I began to think that putting a life together was much like the work I was doing. It's trial and error. It's wanting to do something and having to experiment until you know how. It's making mistakes that can't be undone, like sawing a board too short.

I've decided that life is experimental. You simply learn by living and doing. And since no one has perfect judgment or all prior knowledge, some things will be done wrong and others right.

In the end, I don't think God judges us on how much right or wrong we've done, but on whether or not we've used all these experiences to produce something better. It's the finished product (or person) that God is interested in, not how many mistakes it took to get there. Mistakes can be a positive way of finding out something won't work, and successes give you that warm affirmation that something does work so that next time you'll know what to do.

We can rejoice that our God is a God of grace and forgiveness whose great effort has been to help us find the best and make the most of our lives!

# *The Art of Conversation*

The barber was young and hadn't yet learned the art of casual conversation that is the earmark of his profession. "How are you?" he said. "Fine," I replied. (Pause.) "Rainin' outside." "Yep." (Pause.) "How's your car runnin'?" Finally, he struck on something that could carry the conversation a little further, though I've never been too interested in automobile engines. I said there was a skip in the motor, and then we fell silent, having exhausted our conversational tidbits.

It's a pity that so much verbal exchange is on a meaningless level. You hear conversations all around that say little and mean less. I realize that a fair amount of what we say is social exchange and a courtesy and has an important value, but there's a lot of verbal wind blowing that goes nowhere.

We may be in danger of losing the art of good conversation, and, if we do, I will blame much of it on radio and television.

The cardinal rule of radio is not to allow any "dead" time. Keep talking even if you have lost your place; just don't let any silence come forth. Consequently, there's a lot of chatter on radio that is almost inane.

On television, especially on the talk shows, much is said but little is meant. I can't say I blame them. If I told 50 million viewers that I didn't like liver, I'm sure I would get a thousand letters from liver lovers wondering what kind of kook I was and what did I have against the butchers of America. So there's a lot of talk that sounds sincere but says nothing.

Good conversation doesn't have to be personal or deep to be enjoyed: it can just be a mutual exchange that in turn shows the interest two people have in each other. When it is deep, it can be rich and rewarding, leaving not only a residue of good feeling but new thought as well.

I'm for reviving the lost art of good conversation: "How's your motor runnin'?"

# *The Prince of Peace*

The news report referred to them as "Christians," those soldiers who went into the PLO camp in West Beirut and slaughtered men, women, and children.

When a bomb goes off in Northern Ireland, indiscriminately killing whoever happens to be near, it is credited either to "Catholics" or "Protestants."

The death toll runs high in Iran now. The government is killing its own people, particularly those whom they don't think to be loyal. The reporter says the Iranian government is run by the "clergy."

Christian? Protestant? Catholic? Clergy? Are these words we associate with violence and murder? Of course not, but they are words that are being used to identify people who do such things. How can that be?

It would take several lessons in history to understand why this group is called "Christian" and that one "Protestant," etc. These designations are definitely part of the story of violence in Northern Ireland and Lebanon.

Even so, the lessons can be shortened by saying that "Christian," "Protestant," and "Catholic" have come to identify certain cultural groups in those areas and the history of their differences with opposing groups. Unfortunately they have inflicted great suffering upon each other under the name of their religion.

To wonder if Christ would have any part of violence or hatred is to have the answer before the question is asked. That is not my concern. My concern is that the word "Christian," "Catholic," "Protestant," or "Clergy" could be accepted by someone without understanding that it binds them to a Lord and a way of life that will not condone violence and hatred but calls us to live in love, mercy, and peace.

"Oh God, forgive us if in any way the life we live brings disgrace to the life Christ lived and then empower us to be your disciples who bring the good news of your love for the whole world to see and to know. In the name of the Prince of Peace. Amen."

# Go to Heaven!

More than 80,000 people attended the Florida-Georgia football game. With an air of joyful pandemonium, they leaned toward the field shouting "Go Gators," and "Eat 'em up, Dawgs." Amidst that noise and din and above the sound of their collective cries came the voices of two people saying, "You're going to hell! You're going to hell!" and to emphasize it a large sign was held up for all to see.

Several thoughts come to mind when I hear something like that. What pleasure do they get in doing it? Since they don't expect to go, I'm sure there's comfort in thinking they are safe. Also, there seems to be a perverse pleasure in telling people they're going to "get it."

When God finally made Jonah go to Ninevah with that same message, Jonah warmed up to it so that he got mad when the people repented, and he sulked for days. (Read the fourth chapter carefully.)

Why not shout, "You're going to heaven! You're going to heaven!" The Bible mentions heaven 570 times and hell only 53, with the majority of the hell count in the Old Testament. That means the Bible is 11 to 1 more interested in heaven. It would be more in keeping with Christ to use that slogan because his was a loving invitation, not a dire threat.

Then there's hell itself. I'm sure the announcers believe it to be a place of unrelenting pain and punishment that goes on forever. In those 53 mentions of hell, there's some evidence for that, but somehow this image doesn't conform to the kind of person Christ was and the way he described God.

The earthly father may punish me to correct my behavior, but he would never beat or burn me forever. Didn't Jesus say, "What father among you, if his son asked for a fish, will . . . give him a serpent; or if he asks for an egg, will you give him a scorpion? If you then, who are evil, know how to give good gifts to your children, how much more will the heavenly Father give. . ." (Luke 11:11-13).

I'm not arguing against judgment or even some kind of punishment, but I do have trouble with eternal suffering and the gleeful announcement of it.

St. Francis is reported to have said in one of his prayers, "How can I enjoy heaven, Lord, when I know hell exists? Dear Lord, either take pity on the damned and put them in paradise, or let me go down into the inferno and comfort the sufferers. I'll found an order whose purpose will be to descend into the inferno and comfort the damned. And if we can't lighten their pain, will remain at hell ourselves and suffer along with them!"

There's some indication in the Bible that Jesus descended into hell to announce the good news. The tradition is that he went there between Good Friday and Easter morning. That sounds like something he would do (and I like to believe he did), and if so, there's hope for the hopeless.

# Sacred Gifts

Sometimes for personal Bible study, I choose a book that isn't too familiar. Right now, I'm reading Leviticus.

At first, it doesn't seem too inspirational. But as you read on, something of the sacredness of bringing gifts to God begins to come through. For example, the names of the various offerings begin to say something to you, such as, "thank offerings," "peace offerings," "sin offerings," "guilt offerings." Each had its function, and each spoke to a human need or desire.

Then the quality of the offering is described. If an animal, it must be without blemish. If cereal, the flour must be ground fine. From this, you understand that only the best you have is good enough for God—no coarse grain or sickly animals. The gift must also be from the "first fruits" and not the leftovers.

"Thank offerings," "peace offerings," "sin offerings"—each says something about why we should bring gifts to God. "First fruits" and "without blemish" tell us what kind of gifts to give. The standard was one-tenth, and it is still a good one for today. Those who do it are much more blessed than burdened by it.

All this was in ancient times you might say. Yes, it was, and we don't practice our giving like that any more. But the reasons were right! The sense of a sacred offering set aside for the glory of God, giving from the best you have, bringing your gift with thanksgiving, seeking peace and forgiveness.

We don't burn the gifts anymore. We invest them in God's work, praying as we give that they will enable others to understand, as we do, what a good and loving God it is who has given us far, far more than we could ever return.

# Get Started

My friend Pete, who runs the sandwich shop down the street ("The Home of the Camel Rider"), is going to open another place downtown. It isn't that he is gotten rich on this one and is going to start another; it's the need of a large family that is trying to build a new life in this country.

Pete and his brother Joe are Palestinians and are active in their Orthodox Christian church. I see the priest often in their place, and they show me the same courteous respect they give him, including the title "Father." (None of this "Reverend" or "Preacher" stuff!)

Today, Pete told me about the new place downtown. "I'm a little worried, Father," he said, "because we can't afford to lose; we must succeed." I tried to say some encouraging things to him about his good service and good prices and that I felt sure he'd make a go of it and Joe would carry on well here. He'd talked to the priest about it, he said, and the priest told him, "Clean your heart, get started, and God will help you!"

Oh, how I wish I'd said that. How direct. How straight to the mark. How free of all the analytical clutter we wade through trying to make an important decision. How applicable to almost any significant thing you want to do.

How often we become paralyzed trying to make some important decision by dragging in everything but the kitchen sink, looking at every possible reason why we should or shouldn't, taking first one position and then another until, by default, the action is not taken.

How's your spiritual health? Does your marriage need help? Are you proud of the moral life you lead? Does something important need attention? Then clean your heart, get started, and God will help you!

# *Deer Tracks in Church*

Deer tracks in the church? Who'd ever expect to see something like that? But there they are plain as day, two little fawn prints. Not far away is another print of a more mature deer. Since seeing those, I've been searching for others and have found equine tracks that look like those of a small horse or donkey.

Perhaps you think the strain of this Christmas season has already scrambled my senses and that maybe I am looking for signs that Santa Claus and the holy family have come and gone through the church. No, that's not it; those tracks are molded in the flagstone of the sanctuary and on the walks around the church. They were left there thousands of years ago when the stone was hard enough to walk on but soft enough to leave prints of the animals that passed over it. They are ancient prints of living things that are now permanently enshrined in the church.

Not visible but just as real and more alive are the shaping influences of our forefathers and foremothers whose faith left indelible prints on the church and us. That's not poetic fancy; it's strong stuff set in stone. What they found in their faithful lives and what God gave them along the way, they have left us as a legacy, a treasure to be preserved and passed on so that such knowledge and experience can clarify the faith and point the way for us and others.

This Christmas, I am going to proclaim the birth of Christ again and call us all to strengthen our faith and discipleship, but I shall do so with the awareness that "we are surrounded by so great a cloud of witnesses" who have brought us to this time and place and given us a goodly heritage. I thank God for the faithful who have gone on before us. I pray that we shall continue on until "every knee should bow. . .and every tongue confess that Jesus Christ is Lord, to the glory of God."

# Stray Cats and Cockroaches

Stray cats and cockroaches. Who'd have thought I'd be talking to them? This will need some explanation, so I'll get started.

Several years ago, we bought a small abandoned church at Cedar Key and made a cottage out of it. At the time, there were a lot of roaches on the inside and nearly as many stray cats underneath. I managed to get most of the roaches out, and all of the cats left except one, a pretty calico female. In time, I called the cat "Lucille." I chose that name because she always came back. No matter how seldom I go there, Lucille appears purring and rubbing against my leg. I call her that to help redeem the name from the song, "You picked a fine time to leave me, Lucille." Well, Lucille the cat always comes back and brings the four hungry kids! I seldom see the kittens but hear them in the nearby bushes where she leaves them. Lucille and I have an arrangement when there are fish to clean; I keep the fillets, and she gets the back-bones. I throw them over to her, and, after devouring one or two, she starts carrying them over to the bushes.

Now in reference to the conversation, it started when we were dividing up the fish, and I told her how nice it was to be greeted so cordially when I came and asked how many kids does she have this time.

When the fish were cleaned, I decided to remove a brick pile that had been there too long. Lo and behold, here were all the roaches I had run out of the house! They are the kind that let off a terrible odor when disturbed. In fact, two can make the pulp mill smell like it's turning out Chanel No. 5. So I said, "Look guys, I'm sorry to bother you again, but if you promise not to go back in the house, you can build a condominium with these bricks and rent it out for the winter and I won't complain."

Anyone who talks to cats and cockroaches may be going crazy. I wasn't. I felt contentment. I saw that home in God's created world and marveled at all the creatures that inhabited it. I really didn't expect either to answer though I suspect Lucille would come closer to knowing she was being addressed. Mostly, I just wanted to say:

"This is my father's world,
and to my listening ears

all nature sings,
and 'round me rings
the music of the spheres."

# *Violets Are Blue*

The violets came today. They come every year about this time. They are large and long stemmed, the kind that grow in the hammocks where it's damp and shaded.

We've been getting them for more than 30 years now. They come carefully wrapped in foil and plastic and survive the mail surprisingly well. We receive them because people who knew us then, remember and love us now.

It all started when I was a student pastor and Ellzey Church was my first full-time appointment. I would drive there Sunday morning and stay through the day for the night service.

The woods are beautiful in Levy County, and often times Emily Ann and I would explore them. (We were not married then, and it was a good chance to get off by ourselves. You can't always tell what a preacher's up to between services!)

In the springtime, those woods are covered in wild violets with colors that run from deep purple to pale blue. Ever since childhood, wild violets have had a special excitement for me. And then, in the beginning of my ministry and with the girl I would marry, that meant even more. We picked bunches of them and, after we married, transplanted some to a flower box on the porch of our upstairs apartment.

One dear lady down there remembers, and the violets come every year in the mail. When they arrive, they remind me of a little church and a small congregation who loved and encouraged us into the ministry; of a girl whom I loved then and do now; of woods and wildflowers that God gave us to enjoy. They remind me of the past that tells me who I am and where I came from. They link me to loving people and places who did then and do now nourish my body and soul. This year's bouquet was beautiful. I look forward to the ones to come.

# No Jargon Needed

I just stumbled over a big word in the dictionary that took several tries to pronounce and more than that to spell: ankyloglosia. It means "tongue-tied." How appropriate! Pronouncing the word produces the very condition it describes.

There are some theological words like that. Eschatological is one, better yet, eschatological apocalypticism. They refer to the end of the world, and by the time you've learned to pronounce them, there's a good chance it will have arrived.

The above are, of course, jargon—learned and technical words that are important to scholars and describe times or conditions without lengthy detail and elaboration. They are important to careful study and examination but not necessary to be a participant. That is, you could have a speech impediment without knowing what ankyloglosia was, or the end of the world might come before you could say "eschatological apocalypticism!"

I'm working my way towards the point that a person can be a Christian in the fullest and finest sense without knowing all of its theological language or unraveling each of its doctrines. They are important but not ultimately so.

Jesus said, "You shall love the Lord your God with all your heart, and with all your soul, and with all your strength, and with all your mind; and your neighbor as yourself" (Luke 10:27). This is what is of supreme importance. You may never get all the doctrines explained or the words pronounced properly, but if you live like that, the rest will take care of itself.

# *Touching Life Deeply*

It was his first Communion (and his last). The tumor was growing and was beginning to cause paralysis on his right side. He had been busy getting everything in order: business, personal, and family affairs. He had even gone to the funeral home to make arrangements for his burial. He had come to church a couple weeks before to talk about his service. "Nothing mournful," he said, "and, if you don't mind, I'd like the music to be jazz, if that's okay in the church."

What kind of person can face his own death this way, I wondered. How could he look at it so clear eyed and yet keep his composure, as well as a gentle sense of humor?

"The love of my family," was his answer. "I was lying in bed this morning thinking that heaven is supposed to be such a wonderful place, and I believe it is, but I can't imagine anything better than what I'm feeling right now from those who love me."

The people at the hospice helped too. They taught him how to make the most of the life he had left and to get things in order before he died.

And then there was God, or rather, there was God all along. In the most marvelous way, God had moved into Tim's life. The quiet spirit of God was so evident in him that I felt I, too, was in God's presence.

He asked for Holy Communion, so we went to the altar together. I read every word of the service because I wanted us to hear all of those great assurances. Never did they sound so full of power, grace, and goodness. With the bread and wine in our hands, we were suspended between heaven and earth. I know we were.

Never has Communion meant more to me, nor can I recall taking it with someone so ready to enter God's house.

Tim was buried shortly afterwards, much sooner than we had expected, but everything was in order because he had seen it to himself before he died.

How can a person handle his own death so well? By the love of God, the love of a good wife, the love of family and friends, the help of many fine people at the hospice, and the rare courage of the young man who was determined to live every moment of his life before he died! And Tim did. "It's been the best year of my life," he said. "I don't want to die now, but I wouldn't take anything for this year."

He lived before he died! He found the depth and meaning of life both with God and the people who were near him.

I'm convinced if you touch life that deeply you can give up your earthly existence because you have tasted life eternal and aren't afraid to surrender your body to the grave.

As I went into the sanctuary for his service, I saw him in my mind's eye as a young man standing on the edge of a turbulent river that had to be crossed. Courageously he plunged in, swam across, and reaching the other side, turned and waved with an exuberant smile as much as to say, "It's all right; it can be done; you will make it, too."

# *Sheer Encouragement*

The books of J. R. R. Tolkien and C. S. Lewis have been widely read in the last few years. Tolkien was the author of *The Hobbit*, *Lord of the Rings*, and several other stories of delightful fantasy. Lewis is best known for his books on the Christian faith, such as *Mere Christianity* and *The Screwtape Letters*.

Tolkien and Lewis were teachers of English literature at Oxford University and lifelong friends, but, before they met, Lewis was not a Christian, and Tolkien had no intention of publishing his stories.

What we know them best for now was the result of their mutual encouragement. Lewis persuaded Tolkien to publish his work, and Tolkien helped Lewis find his faith. Later on, Tolkien said, "The unpayable debt I owe to him was not 'influence' as it is ordinarily understood, but sheer encouragement."

What a gift to give someone. What a wonderful, miraculous thing to bring the best out of other people by encouraging them to see and claim their own talents and possibilities.

As I write this, two things come to mind. First, encouragement is in short supply; you don't see or hear too much of it. Second, it is the finest and most fertile way to help someone grow, discover himself or herself, and enjoy life. Add one more: there's nothing complicated about encouragement. A simple, honest compliment will do the job and have far-reaching effect.

The Bible refers to Barnabas as the "Son of Encouragement" (Acts 4:36). What a wonderful way to be remembered. We could all be sons or daughters of encouragement. It wouldn't take much time or effort just see something in someone and compliment it. Do it everyday, and it will become a delightful habit. The best place to begin is at home.

# See You at the Dance

"She took dancing lessons when she was 97," he said. "Dancing lessons at 97!" I replied. "I'm going to talk to her daughters about this." And so I did.

"Yes," one of them said, "she always wanted to learn to dance, so she took lessons and had a wonderful time. We bought her dancing shoes. One pair was red and the other black. She liked the red ones best."

I wanted to know more. Childhood had been hard and harsh. Somehow the determination to make the most and find the best in life had given her a sense of humor, joy, and excitement. It made her tolerant, understanding, and appreciative of people. It gave her the desire to live life to the fullest. So, at 92, she visited as many of the states as she could, and, at 97, she took dancing lessons.

I keep telling myself you don't have to get sluggish or grouchy as you get older. You can go places and do things you didn't have time for when younger.

If I'm around at 97, I hope to see you at the dance.

# *The Power of Prayer*

Did you ever wonder if those written prayers you recite in church have any effect? They do, and I can tell you how I know.

We live in a high-rise continuing care community known as Lutheran Towers. When the Lutherans built it, they created a beautiful sanctuary for worship on the top floor. Regular services are held there each Sunday, and it remains open at all times for meditation and prayer.

Last week, I had a sense of anxiety that I wanted to pray about, so I decided to go up to the sanctuary and sit quietly quoting to myself that part of the 46th Psalm that says, "Be still and know that I am God." This, I felt, would bring a sense of peace and awareness of God. On the way in, I saw a stack of last Sunday's worship programs, and, for some reason, which I can't explain, I picked one up. As I sat down, I began to read the congregation's printed "Prayers of Intercession." It is a beautiful prayer that includes the earth, the nations of the world, and a number of things that concern us all. In the midst of that lovely prayer were the words "for those who are anxious." "That's me!" I said to myself. "They were all praying for me, and here I am, sitting in the church feeling the power of their prayer and being blessed by it."

I have no idea how prayer works, but I know it does. I don't know how written and recited prayers reach the prayed for, but I know they do because I felt surrounded and blessed by this congregation who said in unison: "We pray for those who are anxious." In addition to the words of the congregation, the pastor closed by saying, "May the peace of the Lord be with you always." These words, too, felt real and personal.

I said that I didn't know how prayer works, but God does. He becomes the conduit of our concern and, thus, our prayers, personal or those in a written or recited liturgy. They find their way to the intended person or purpose. I know; I felt the power of the prayer of the people in this congregation.

# Love Is Blind

The ministry is a second career for me. The first was operating a sawmill. When people ask what inspired me to go into the ministry, I often tell them it was the sawmill. Saw milling is mostly back-breaking, hard labor that doesn't pay very much. The sawmill hands, as they were called, usually worked there because they weren't skilled at much else.

The log turner was Elmer. Elmer was illiterate. He wasn't ignorant, but he was illiterate, and he was always bragging about his wife. "I don't know what that woman sees in me," he would say. "She could have married anybody she wanted, but she married me." And whenever he would say that, the rest of the crew would always chime in and say, "We sure don't know what she sees in you either, Elmer. You're ugly, you stink (we all did), and you've got dirt and pine tar all over you." Their teasing never seemed to stop him from bragging about his wife.

None of us had ever seen his wife. We saw his two children now and then, a boy and a girl. They would stop by after school to see Elmer or to bring his lunch if they were out of school. They were always neatly dressed and well mannered. He bragged about them a good bit too because they were doing so well in school.

Judging from the children and what Elmer said about his wife, I had an image of her as a person better educated and more cultivated than he, but she loved him and married him and gave him a good home and two fine children.

One day, a man showed up at the mill and said he represented the government. He was asking about workers' compensation, withholding tax, and some other things we hadn't given much thought about. He wasn't pleased that we didn't have this information, but if we'd get busy right then and get the names and social security numbers of all of the workers, he might not be as hard on us as he could be.

When I asked Elmer for this information, he said that I would have to get it from his wife. Under the urgency of the situation, I ran to his house and knocked on the door. When the door opened, I was stunned! Even now, I pray that my face did not betray my feelings. I had never seen a face so disfigured before. She gave me the information that I asked for. I thanked her and walked back to the mill wondering what this was all about, this continual boasting of Elmer about his wife. I thought about it then and later on and came to the realization it was about love. They loved each other. And because they did, she saw past his illiteracy to a good and loving man, and he couldn't see her distorted face for the beauty of her spirit.

When I returned, Elmer didn't act as though I'd seen something I shouldn't, nor did he stop his bragging. The only thing that changed was that I joined in with the others when he said that he couldn't understand why she married him. "I don't understand it either, Elmer. You're ugly, you stink, and you're covered with dirt and pine tar."

Later on when I learned more about the love of God, I realized that Elmer and his wife had a spark of the great love God has for all of us. God sees what little we know and how illiterate we are about Him. Just as easily, He sees our distorted lives, what the Bible calls sin, but His love looks beyond to the man or woman He knows us to be, and God loves that person so dearly that He doesn't see those things.

"Love bears all things, believes all things, hopes all things, and endures all things! Love never ends" (I Corinthians 13:7-8).

# *Love not Fear*

A few years ago, I became acquainted with the Persian poet Hafiz (1320-1329) who is among those mystical writers knows as Sufis. Though they may be called mystics, there is nothing hidden or cloudy about their writings; they always seem so accurate and to the point in illuminating human and divine matters.

Here's something I recently read from Hafiz: "It is a great injustice and a monumental act of cruelty for any religion to make someone fear God." This made me think back to our religious past when fear was the stock in trade of the traveling evangelist and many others who didn't travel. Their invitation to come to Christ was often accompanied by what would happen if you didn't. Fear was a very prominent part of their invitation to come to Jesus.

I often wondered how you could teach someone to love through using fear or by describing the punishment that they would receive if they didn't.

When you start searching the Bible for the word fear, you will find it everywhere. And if you want to see fear in action, read the Book of Revelation. How do we reconcile this with Hafiz's statement and my cherished belief? All I can tell you is how I deal with it.

The heart and soul of Christianity is that Jesus is an authentic reflection of God; to know what Jesus is like is to know what God is like. His teachings and actions reveal the ways of God among us. Since I believe this, I turn to his words and actions to look for fear, threat, violence, and rejection. I don't find it. The one continuous operative word there is love.

Three of the four gospels tell the story of Jesus walking on water, but that's not the end of the story nor the message of the story. The end of the story is when Jesus approaches his fearful disciples in the midst of a storm, and the message of the story is, "Don't be afraid; it is I." Here is where my faith rests.

One further word: "There is no fear in love, for perfect love casts out fear" (1 John 4:18).

# God's Song

We were surrounded by music in the dining room of Bethune-Cookman College. Their marvelous choir had come to sing for us. Not only were we surrounded, but their voices also permeated the room when they moved among our tables as they sang. Suddenly, those powerful voices stopped. For a brief second, the silence was as strong as the music. Then a soft, sweet solo voice could be heard. It didn't last long, just enough time to find the singer in the crowd. I noticed that she was leaning as though about to fall and trying to catch her balance. In fact, that was the case, for just as she finished singing, two strong men stepped forward, took her beneath the arms, and gently led her out, probably to a wheelchair. It all happened so quickly that it took a moment to understand what was happening. They helped her sing her song. She had a lovely song to sing, but, without someone's help, we could not have heard it.

There's a story behind that, too. She wanted to sing; the choral director said, "Sure, we have a place for you," and the more able said, "We'll see that you get there and get back." And we heard her sing her song.

Before I became a minister and most every day since, I've had this continuing question: "Lord, what would you have me to do?" One answer that has come clearer over the years is, "Help them sing their song."

If every person is a creation of God, and if each is a unique person with a life to live, then within this uniqueness are talents and gifts to be enjoyed and shared. I have felt God saying, "First, you must recognize and acknowledge that they are my people and, then, as you are able, help them find themselves and their gifts in me." I don't know how well I've done that, but I believe it's my calling and yours as well.

When I think of the countless people who have encouraged me and opened doors for me, I know without them I would not be able to sing my song, such as it is, nor would I have had much chance to join the choir.

# The Simple Faith of Street Ed

My first assignment from seminary was to the First United Methodist Church in Chiefland, Florida. We arrived there in June 1954 and found the parsonage; it faced highway U.S. 19, which passed through the center of town. No one was there when we arrived, so we got busy unpacking our few belongings.

The first real visitor came the next morning with a knock on the door. Standing there was a kind, gentle looking black man with an aging face. He handed me the morning paper and said he wanted to welcome us to town. He told me that he loved the Lord and all the preachers in town. I thanked him, and he went on his way. We saw him the next morning and the next as he passed the house picking up trash along the highway as it went north. An hour or so later, we saw him coming back on the other side of the highway doing the same thing. I was told that he had taken it upon himself to do this and, after picking up trash in both directions, would return to the one block business district and sweep the sidewalks. So far as I knew, no one paid him to do this, but the druggist provided him lunch, and the owner of the dry goods store kept him in clothes. No one mistreated him, and everyone seemed to respect and appreciate what he did for the town.

His name was was Ed Henderson, and the people there referred to him as Street Ed. When I asked his age, he gave me a date in the 1930s. "You're older than that, aren't you?" I replied. "Oh yes," he said, "but that's when I was born of God."

Some accident of birth had made Ed less mentally able than some people, but he was neither dumb nor stupid. In fact, I came to believe that he understood more and did more with what he understood than many of us who had more talents but made less use of them.

In addition to keeping the town clean, Ed had other interesting things that he did; for example, he would write on the sidewalk with a large blue crayon. The messages were important, such as, "School is starting. Watch out for children." And down at the end of the sidewalk where part of it was broken, he wrote, "Watch Your Step." Occasionally, he would inscribe the title of a movie that was playing at the local theater. Once, when the feature was something like Honky Tonk Babes behind Bars (We always got Hollywood's best.), Ed, always the gentleman, wrote, "See the Ladies in Jail."

One time, when I went downtown to the bank, I noticed in large blue letters just to the right of the front door, "God made me. Ed." That's when I knew that Ed understood much more than many of us where life came from and how it was to be lived—in service to others.

The railroad cut diagonally across U.S. 19 just south of the business block, and, where it did, there was a small triangular plot of ground. There were two or three mounds there, graves for the canine friends that followed Ed as he went up and down the highway. In addition, Ed hung a lighted lantern there at night. When I asked him why the lantern was there, he replied that the Bible said, "Let the light so shine before men that they may see your good works and glorify your Father who is in heaven." Oftentimes when returning home after dark and seeing Ed's lantern, I would remember why God had given us our lives and how we ought to live them.

The Russian Orthodox Church has a tradition of the Holy Fool. These are people who in some odd way call attention to the faith by wandering about in strange dress or repeating some scripture or spiritual statement over and over. They aren't fools, just different, and they stand apart from society in some demonstrable way to call attention to God. In the finest sense of the word, Ed was a holy fool.

"If anyone among you thinks he is wise in this age, let him become a fool that he may become wise. For the wisdom of this world is folly with God" (I Corinthians 3: 18-19).

# The Last Shall Be First

I suspect "the world's oldest profession" is not only the oldest but the most universally plied and can be found in every clime and territory. Thus, our little rural town had its own "shady lady." Her name was Miss Lizzy, and she was in her mid-forties.

Miss Lizzy lived on a country road about three or four miles out of town with her mother and an adolescent boy whom she said was her brother. She was not a local beauty, far from it, and a heavy layer of cosmetics didn't hide the fact; it only made it worse. Whenever Miss Lizzy came into town, the young men liked to tease each other by saying, "Miss Lizzy is in town looking for you. She says that you owe her some money." That always brought a lot of laughter and finger pointing.

Word went around town one day that Miss Lizzy's mother had died, and, as local pastor, I went out to see her. I need to pause here to say that I've always liked some of those old-time Southern gospel songs, the kind that come from the simple faith of rural folks. I'm not talking about that choreographed stuff you hear on the radio or television that they call "country music." I'm talking about the real thing, such as "Life Is Like a Mountain Road," "May the Circle Be Unbroken," and "Tell Mother I'll Be There." Such songs have provided a lot of pleasure and laughter for me and still do, and, for a while, when anyone asked for a song request, I would call out "sing 'Mother's Not Dead She's Only Sleeping!'"

Parking my car in Miss Lizzy's yard was understood and acceptable that day; any other time would have caused a lot of talk and speculation. After receiving my condolences for her mother's death, Miss Lizzy said that she felt comforted by the words of the old hymn "Mother's Not Dead She's Only Sleeping." Those words were a fit description of her feelings, and I vowed never to make fun of them again.

A mile or so down the road from Miss Lizzy, an elderly woman lived alone in a small house. Some of my parishioners who lived in the area said her name was Mrs. Nash. She was an invalid, they said, and no one seemed to be taking care of her. They did her grocery shopping and picked up her medicines, but so far as they knew, no one else came by. And then they asked if I would stop by to see her now and then.

Whenever I would go out to see Mrs. Nash, she would always be sitting out on her small front porch very neat and tidy. I wondered how she managed, in her condition, to take such good care of herself but didn't dare ask. I learned not to pry after the day she counted out $5.70 in nickels, dimes, and quarters and asked me to take her tithe to the church for her. The amount of her gift told me that her monthly income was $57.00. "Mrs. Nash," I said, "You need that money for yourself. Why don't you just keep it?" "I didn't ask you what to do with it," she said. "I asked you to take it to the church for me." Later when I poured the coins into an offering plate and placed them on the altar, I better understood what the Bible calls "A fragrant offering, acceptable to the Lord."

One day, the sheriff's office called to say that Mrs. Nash was found dead and could I come to help identify her. The only people at the house were the sheriff, a couple of funeral home attendants, and Miss Lizzy, who was crying. For the sheriff and attendants, it was just another routine death, but Miss Lizzy was all broken up about it. Later, I learned why. Every night, just before dark, Miss Lizzy went down to Mrs. Nash's house to bathe her and get her ready for bed, and every morning, she came back to get her up and dressed and out on the porch. That's why Mrs. Nash always looked so nice; Miss Lizzy saw to it! And that is why she was so broken up; another person who was dear to her had died.

The funeral was a simple graveside service. Hardly anyone was there. I was hoping Miss Lizzy would come so that at least one person would be there to mourn Mrs. Nash's death, but she didn't attend too many public gatherings like that.

Some years later, I was back in that little town and asked someone whatever happened to Miss Lizzy. "The last I heard," he said, "was that she was teaching Sunday school in some little church around here."

The teachings of Jesus quite often turn common opinions on their head. Such sayings as, "The first shall be last and the last shall be first." And then there's the one about harlots and tax collectors going into the kingdom of God ahead of the righteous. That one is hard to take if you're busting your behind trying to be religious and doing everything right only to find that harlots and tax collectors are ahead of you in the line to heaven.

I was glad to hear that Miss Lizzy finished her years teaching Sunday school. I'm sure there were some things that she didn't tell the children for the sake of their innocence and just maybe to protect the reputation of some of the church leaders.

Somehow, I could hear Miss Lizzy in those later years humming and singing to herself "Tell Mother I'll Be There."

# Our Final Words

On July 24, 2002 in Somerset County, Pennsylvania, a sudden disaster happened in the Quecreek coal mine. That morning, two teams of nine men each had gone into the mine and began work in separate areas. Unknown to them, team one was working the the area of an old mine shaft, and when they drilled into it, water came pouring out on them. It came with such force and quantity that they were trapped and couldn't get out of the mine. The story of their rescue, which was a marvel of human effort, could be told many times over about how people at their best will forget about themselves to come to the aid of others.

It took 77 hours to get those men out, and, all the while that this frantic effort was taking place above ground, another drama was taking place beneath. That is the one I want to tell you about because it, too, is an example of human beings at their best.

You will remember there were two crews working in different places. When the water burst through, the first thing team one did was to call team two and warn them about the water. The next thing they did was to seek a higher place in the mine, which cut off the possibility of escape. After hours had passed and they realized there was little possibility of rescue, they began to discuss how they would die. They prayed then and agreed that they would die together. A long rope was found among their gear, and this was to be used to tie one to the other. They wished to leave farewell messages for their families, so they found some soggy cardboard, and each person had a piece to write a few words. Someone produced a dinner pail, and their messages were placed in it with the hopes it would be found later. When anyone was in danger of hypothermia, they huddled together to keep him warm. They kept encouraging one another though there was little hope.

These men were trapped for more than three days until finally the people above located them and drilled down to bring them up one by one. Their rescue was, indeed, a miraculous story. But it was the way the miners faced life and death and cared for each other that I wanted to share with you. It was those last words that were written to their families that were so significant to me. I wonder what they said as a last message to their loved ones and if they gave them the message when they got out.

What kind of message would you leave in the dinner pail for those you love? It might be a good idea to tell them before the flood waters come.

# The Church and the Town Square

In the summer of my sophomore year at college, I volunteered for a nationwide service project of the United Methodist Church. For the most part, these student teams were sent to work in large cities, but mine went to Iowa to conduct Bible schools in small rural churches. Arrangements had been made for us to stay at a local college and go from there each day to our church assignments.

I arrived a few days early and spent my time wandering about the small county seat town that reminded me of Tarpon Springs, Florida. Before WW II, Tarpon Springs was "town" for several small communities around it, mine among them. That was where the grocery stores, barbershops, doctors, and dentists were located and where folks from the surrounding fruit groves and fishing villages came for these services, especially on Saturdays.

It was more than just buying groceries and getting haircuts. It was time for people to meet and greet, to share work problems and family stories, for the kids to go to the movie theater and the ice cream parlor. It was a delightful flow of humanity, most of whom knew each other. This Iowa town served the same purpose, and I knew there was something familiar about it that I liked.

Now fast forward to the project. We left each morning for an assigned church to conduct Bible school with all of those wonderful farm kids. There was one in the morning, one at lunch, and another one in the afternoon. Saturday morning was for washing clothes, writing letters, and taking care of other personal needs. Saturday afternoon was a trip to the lake or some other recreational area. Saturday night, we were to prepare ourselves spiritually to return to those churches and conduct services. Here's how that went: We were told to walk quietly across campus to the chapel, sit quietly while proceeding through the long form of the communion service, receive communion, and walk quietly across campus back to the dorm. I did that the first week, but the second week after communion, I walked quietly across campus and quietly to town. I joined the kids at the ice cream parlor and walked around the square seeing all of those people. It was Tarpon Springs all over again.

I didn't mean to seduce any of the other students, but a few found out, and for a time, a small shadowy group slipped off campus and went to town. One morning, the director called everyone together and with a stern voice said, "There is someone who has not been going back to the dorm after the communion service but going into the town." I didn't want to give him a chance to say any more, so I stood and said, "I'm the one who is doing it, and all I've got to say is that there's a lot more going on in the town square than there is in the communion service."

That happened in the summer of 1949, and here we are today debating something similar. Where does the church belong? What is its primary task? It is important for the church to be at worship and to receive communion, but it needs to go straight from there to the town square. It's the town square where the church needs to declare and demonstrate the good news of God's love.

# Hospice and Hope

I've been going to Hospice for several days now and will keep going for a few more. You might think it is a morbid duty, but it isn't. There's a lot of love to be found at Hospice; it is the love that surrounds the terminally ill by family and friends as well as those from Hospice who serve them. It's warm and genuine and real. Hospice teaches us to be open and accepting of death. And when we do, with love, much of the burden is lifted from the dying as well as the living. Each helps the other to go on with their journey. There is great comfort and strength in this.

I leave more with thoughtfulness than anything else, aware that I too shall die sooner now than later since I'm already past the biblical three score and ten. I want to accept my death as a natural event, something God planned as carefully as my birth. I want to leave with a heart filled with love and thanksgiving. Love for God, love for those special people whose lives are entwined with mine, and, as much as possible, love for all of God's creatures and creation.

I'd like to leave with a sense of expectancy, believing that I was on my way to yet another part of God's marvelous creation, planned for as carefully as was this unknown world I was born into, a world I could not have possibly imagined.

One day on the way to Hospice, I thumbed through Psalms looking for one or more that spoke of life and death. Many of them do with great faith and realism. I came upon the 39th Psalm and found these words speaking to me: "Lord, let me know my end, and what is the measure of my days; let me know how fleeting my life is. . .and now, Lord, for what do I wait? My hope is in thee. Deliver me from all my transgressions. . ."

# *Paying a Debt*

I was in Miami in the early sixties when many Cubans were fleeing the Communist Revolution. A Cuban Methodist pastor who was among them was now serving in Miami. He came one day to say, as he left Cuba, one of his parishioners begged him to take their son with him and they would follow as soon as possible. Five years passed, and finally they were able to get out through Mexico. Could I help financially? It was not a large sum, and I did so gladly.

The day of their arrival, the Cuban family came to see us as though we were responsible for it all. And every Christmas, wherever they were, a Christmas card was sent with many expressions of gratitude.

Years passed, eight or ten I think, when a letter came with an enclosed check:

"Dear Reverend:

Thank you for your letter, we are so glad to hear from you again also.

George is out of town until tomorrow. He went together with Church's youngs to a encampment. He attend Lakewood Methodist Church. Lido and I, we attend Tampa Hights in spanish.

George can not to write this letter for me, but my wife and I are very anxious for send to you this letter soon. I hope that you may understand my deficient English's grammar.

Once, some years ago, that you had given to our dear brother Ornan this dollars for help to us. We are sure that you had forgot this. But we never can not to forget these your nice, beautiful sacrifice for us. Today we are very happy to return to you this material service, with another part of our big debt of gratitude to you, and only we will let that Our Lord do it to you. We have present to you forever in our hearts."

The check that he sent was issued from a loan company.

# *Christmas on Okinawa*

I joined the Navy in 1944, and soon after the war was ended was sent to Okinawa as part of the occupation force. Okinawa was a place of hard fighting. The allies wanted it as a staging place to attack Japan. Consequently, there was terrible fighting and a lot of destruction. Naha, the major city, was rubble.

There were no barracks when we arrived, just tents and Quonset huts (sheet metal buildings that could be put up quickly). My group, who worked at the Fleet Post Office, lived in numbered tents, a short walk from the Quonset huts where the mail was kept and sorted.

Entertainment was sparse, so we made our own.

We saved our weekly Coke or beer ration (four bottles of one or the other) and met on Friday nights in tent 22. There were George and Shorty, Bob and Pop, Whitey and me, and several others whose names I don't recall. The rule was that everyone had to do something entertaining whether he knew how or not. That was easy for Bob, an accordion player who had his accordion. There was another fellow who played his sax. The rest of us were left to our own ingenuity, and there wasn't much of that. I did a soft shoe while trying to sing "He's a Yankee Doodle Dandy." (I remembered seeing James Cagney do something like that in a movie.) Pop, a short Italian guy from New York City, waited until last, until he had drunk his four beers and any others he could scrounge. By this time, he was ready for his grand performance: a strip tease! It was ugly; it was awkward; it wasn't anything anyone would want to see. And then the chorus began: "Don't do it, Pop! Nobody wants to see you naked!" "Stop it, Pop! You're ruining the party!"

Christmas Eve was a most memorable time. It could have been that the drink ration was enlarged a little because of Christmas. Bob and the sax man were playing carols, and we were singing at the top of our voices. Pop felt sentimental and started crying. Somewhere, among those long rows of tents, a loud voice said, "Shut up that damn noise!" Someone from tent 22 stepped out and said, "Shut your damn mouth!" Things were quiet for a moment, and then an automatic rifle began to unload its clip across the top of tent 22. From then on, it was Silent Night all the way.

# Pulse

Yesterday morning, we awoke to the news of a shooting at a gay nightclub called Pulse a few blocks from where we live in downtown Orlando. Forty-nine people were dead and that many more taken to the hospital.

Awakening to that kind of news was too much to comprehend. A day has passed, and I still haven't taken it all in: more than 100 people dead and dying lying all over the floor. I can't visualize the scene much less imagine the fear and horror that each person must have felt. We are told it is the worst such act in the history of the United States. That will give you some sense of it.

Theories and explanations are already being offered as to why the shooter did it. Some are saying it is because he is a Muslim (though born in this country) and connected to some violent sect of his faith. So far, no direct connection has been found. What makes more sense to me is what his father and former wife had to say. His father said that the shooter had a deep hatred for gay people. His former wife said that he was abusive and mentally ill. Put those things together, and you have someone quite capable of such a horrible act.

It's this condemnation of gay people that I want to single out. It's found in his religion and in mine. It is in his culture and in mine. As a result, many homosexual people have had to live in hiding and in denial of their real selves. Because of this widespread prejudice, many bigoted or deranged people took it as license to do any abusive or violent thing they chose to gay people.

I want to pause here and say that I have reached the conclusion that we are what we are because we were born this way: female, male, transgender, homosexual, or whatever may be our physical or emotional makeup. It isn't a choice; it's a given. To blame anyone for who he is is to blame you or me for who we are.

The history of our nation has many tragic stories of the killing of Native Americans and African Americans because they were considered inferior, dirty, ignorant, or violent. *The New York Times* recently reviewed a book entitled *An American Genocide*. It was about the mass slaughter of Native Americans in California. The author said, "The slaughter of California Indians was rapid and thorough even by the grim standards prevailing elsewhere in North America."

In my first rural parish, I learned of a mob attacking a black community in our county. A written account said, "Every home owned by a Negro was burned to the ground. When the homes were set on fire, if any inhabitants were hiding inside, they were shot as they ran to get away from the hot flames." It was still in the memory of the old timers, and some I knew well enough to ask about it. One friend said that he was a boy at the time, and when some of the mob came to his town, they gave him a matchbox with a black finger in it. Because it was recent in memory, I spent a lot of time gathering information about it. I learned it began with a rumor (never proved) that a black man had raped a white woman. This was all that was needed to gather a mob of 200 or 300 and burn the town, killing many of its residents.

You might say that these stories about Native Americans and African Americans aren't to be compared with what happened here to homosexuals, but I say they are; the mindset and motivation for violence against them came from the same source: the denigration and devaluation of other human beings. When that's done, most anything can happen.

# *The Power of Imperfection*

I once read a biography of a fine and famous person. The author did not try to make him larger than life, nor did he seek to hide his flaws. He presented him as a talented, devoted man who also had some odd and peculiar habits that no one quite understood.

After looking closely at someone's life, you might say, "Well, he wasn't so great after all. Look at all those quirks in his personality. He's just like the rest of us." Of course he's just like the rest of us! He had strengths and weaknesses, virtues and talents just like everyone else. The test of greatness is not whether a person has any flaws but how far beyond them he is able to go, what he can accomplish in spite of them.

The great personalities of the Bible are not presented to us as pure and perfect; their sins and failures are revealed as well as their noble qualities. Perhaps the greatest biblical story that illustrates this is the story of David and Bathsheba (II Samuel 11-12). King David had so wanted for his wife the beautiful Bathsheba whom he'd impregnated that he arranged for her husband to be killed in battle. Great grief and sorrow were the result of this as well as the loss of their child. "Then David consoled his wife Bathsheba. . .and she bore him a son and David named him Solomon. The Lord loved Solomon." From this human tragedy came a greater King David and their famous son, Solomon. The Bible understands that "All have sinned and fall short of the glory of God," but it goes on to say, "They are justified by his grace as a gift through the redemption which is in Christ Jesus" (Romans 3:23).

The joy of it all is what God can do with imperfect people.

# Our Awareness of God

Several years ago, a dear Catholic friend introduced me to Michael Morwood, both personally as well as his writings. Morwood was a Catholic priest; I say was because he was told the beliefs and opinions expressed in his books were not acceptable to the church. His choice, therefore, was to stop writing or give up the priesthood. He chose the latter.

I've already read his books *God Is Near*; *Faith, Hope, and a Bird Called George*; and now I'm into *In Memory of Jesus.*

Here are some of his major thoughts: God is with us here, now. God is not in some far away place called heaven where, if you are good enough, you will go some day. This is what he refers to as the "elsewhere" God. Much of our religious conversation and music represent this kind of "elsewhere" God, but it's not so, says Morwood. God is with us here, now. Furthermore, God is within us, not outside of us.

Both of these are important ideas, and they make my faith experience much more real and personal. I don't have to seek for God anywhere but here, nor do I need to look beyond myself to find God. Frankly, there is nothing new or strange about these ideas; they are in the Bible and very much a part of the teachings and activities of Jesus. Morwood simply untangles a lot of biblical language and theological verbiage from around them and makes them plain to us. A good way to find this demonstrated is to imaginatively join the crowds who followed Jesus and see how he speaks and acts with people. He reflects the God who is near, and when he spoke, "the people heard him gladly," which means ordinary people like us heard and understood.

I think that we need awareness more than anything else—awareness that God is here, now and that God dwells in us. And, if you want to learn more about God's presence here and now, try meditating on how lovable you are to God, not how unlovable you might think you may be to yourself, but how much God loves you. I'm thinking that, if we did that for long, God's nearness and closeness would begin to make themselves felt. The interesting thing about finding that you are loved just for being yourself is that you want to be more and to do more for the One who loves you.

If you want to know more about what Morwood has to say, read his little book *Faith, Hope, and a Bird Called George.* If you don't like big books, you will like this one. It's only six inches tall and a half inch thick, but don't let the title or the size fool you; it has much to say.

# God in Nature

Recently, I attended the ordination service of a friend in the Bahamas. His parish includes Harbor Island, the mainland of Eleuthera, and a small church on Current island. Having completed all of his educational requirements and successfully served his churches for two years, he was ready for full ordination.

A friend made her beach cottage available, and I enjoyed staying on one of the most beautiful beaches in the Bahamas. In fact, I think the beaches of Eleuthera are often on the list of the world's most beautiful beaches. One reason for its beauty is the pink sand. There is a coral reef out beyond the beach that has, for centuries, been sending in bits of pink coral, which eventually has given the beaches that light pink color. It's beautiful.

I awoke early one morning to take a walk and, for a time, was there by myself. I felt alone on that lovely beach with nothing in sight but the vast Atlantic Ocean and no sound but the breaking waves on the shore. A moment like that always gives me a feeling of the grandeur of God's creation and my small part in it. It makes me aware that life is a gift, and I give thanks to God for all creation.

I've always liked to beach comb and do it instinctively. The first thing I saw was a small ball of something with a beautiful azure color. It turned out to be a tangle of netting or fishing line. Next, I picked up what appeared to be a small yellow pebble. It was a piece of plastic. One after another, those colorful things on the beach were not seashells; they were bits and pieces of discarded trash that were thrown into the sea somewhere and found their way to one of the world's beautiful beaches.

People have been warning us over and over that we are polluting our seas and trashing our beaches and that we must stop before the world becomes a vast garbage dump and our air too foul to breathe. Already, pure water has become a problem in some places.

The biblical view of the world is that "the earth is the Lord's and the fullness thereof and they and all who dwell therein." It also considers us to be caretakers of the world. We are to use what we need, leave something for others, and protect what is left for all.

Polluting and protecting aren't the same thing, but they are closely connected. If we don't stop using our natural resources indiscriminately and dumping our waste where we want, the generations ahead will find themselves short of resources and living in a garbage dump. These are the thoughts that came to me as I walked along one of the world's most beautiful beaches picking up plastic trash.

# What We're Called to Do

My first trip to the Bahamas came from the invitation of Rev. William Makepeace who asked a pastor friend and me to travel to the Andros circuit. The year was about 1958. After arriving in Nassau, we flew to Mastic Point then caught a lumber truck to a saw mill at the lumber camp. We preached at the mill church that night and had a song fest with the mill workers. I shall never forget singing, "There will be a meeting in the Air." There was a line in the hymn that said, "there will be no grumblers there." I shouted and asked them to sing it over. I wanted to hear again that there would be "no grumblers there."

The next day, a man took us down the creek to the settlement of Stafford Creek. As we went through the village, he was calling out, "The ministers reach, the ministers reach," so we were properly announced. We had not been at the mission house long when three ladies arrived with food. One set the table, another took the broom and started cleaning, and a third asked if we had any laundry to be washed. We both quickly said we would keep the house clean and could wash our own clothes. I shall never forget their answer, for it was life changing for me. I had become weary of the multitude of responsibilities that pastors have that have little to do with the ministry. I was even wondering if this was what I wanted to do for the rest of my life. Their simple answer focused the task of the ministry for me that day, and I never forgot it. "No!" one them said. "We know how to do those things; we want you to come to our houses and read the Bible and pray with us and go to the church and preach the gospel." THAT'S IT! THAT'S IT! That's what God called me to do, to pray with the people, read the Bible with them, and preach the Gospel: the good news of God. And if I fail to do that, I have failed my calling. From then on, what those ladies told us has been the primary focus of the ministry for me.

# *Protection from Ghosts*

On one of my earliest trips to the Bahamas, I was asked to go to Staniard Creek, a community on the larger island of Andros. The English missionary who asked me to go there had served the community for many years and knew it quite well. We met in Nassau, and, as I was leaving, he laughingly said that the church would be full in the morning but only half filed in the evening. "Why is that?" I asked. "Because the folks believe a ghost is lurking around the crossroad and those who live below it won't pass that way at night, even to go to church. I've chided them about it," he said, "and told them I've never met a ghost there night or day, but their reply was that was because I knew too many texts." It was their belief that if you quoted scripture to ghosts, they won't bother you.

On arrival at Staniard Creek, I found my host was the village nurse and accommodations were to be the clinic. The nurse was a charming person and had prepared a delicious meal not often found in the outer islands at the time. We had fresh fruits and vegetables and, for dessert, a chilled bartlett pear.

We talked well into the night. That's when I became aware that people as well educated as my host didn't always have the opportunity for that kind of conversation, and she was eager to hear what what was going on elsewhere.

It was late when I left to go over to the clinic. As I got up to leave, I jokingly asked if the ghost had ever bothered a visiting minister. She laughed and said she hadn't known of it.

The clinic was a small building on the southwest quadrant of the crossroad. I went over and made ready for bed. Just as I extinguished the light and lay down, a dog howled under the window! For the sake of my soul, the only scripture that I could think of was, "Jesus wept."

# Teamwork

The establishment of the Zion Children's Home is a wonderful story of faith and hope working together and not giving up until the job is done. I don't remember just when it was, but I was at Current Island one day and saw Mrs. Earmily Munroe walking along with a trail of children behind her. I learned later that those were children whom she had volunteered to care for because the social worker could not find homes for them. This loving act is what started the conversation about establishing a home for children in North Eleuthera. The conversation spread among Methodist people and leaders until one day a meeting was called at the Harbour Island manse. Could it be done? Where would we get the land and money? That day, the settlement of Current Island offered the land, and that day Osbourn Weech offered to build it at no charge for his service and only half for his workmen. After making this offer, Osbourn came over and asked, "How much money do you have?" "About $20,000," I replied. "Good," he said, "Let's get started!" And that was the beginning.

An architect in Orlando designed and drew the plans at no charge. A charitable organization in Sanford, Florida sent someone to see the site and confirm the need, then gave $50,000. An individual in Nassau gave this same amount. These are but a few of the gifts that I remember. Churches in the Bahamas and the U.S. began to step forth with labor and money until it was finished, furnished, and landscaped. As of today, many churches, work teams, and youth groups continue to come with help. That's how, when Christian folks want to do something, they get it done.

# *Spiritual Truth*

The preachers' task, in my view, is to be able to speak of spiritual matters to make them understandable and obtainable to the listeners, and that is a very difficult thing to do. First, preachers must have some vision of the thing they wish to tell about and then find words to describe it. Reading the Bible and the great spiritual writers is a good place to begin. Spiritual truth has a way of confirming itself to you so that when you hear or read it you say to yourself yes, that's true; I believe it.

That's a good thing about God's truth. It confirms itself to you, and another thing about it is that it recognizes itself in others. Oftentimes, there is something about the person you just met that tells you that she too is a person of the spirit. The God Spirit in her reaches out to the God Spirit in you.

For me, the discovery of this Spirit is not just in the Bible or great spiritual masters but in writers, poets, and musicians who convey some wonderful universal truth to us. Because I experience this, I find myself underscoring such statements in my books and copying them from magazines or movies with plans to use them in a sermon some time. Since they have spoken so well and clearly to me, I believe they will for a listening congregation.

One thing I believe: The truth of God is not confined to any one religion. Christianity is based on Judaism, and Islam has elements of both. Spiritual leaders of all faiths have a commonality of faith that connects them much closer than popular opinion would think.

I have been reading the Sufi poets lately and marvel at how closely connected they are to my Christian faith. The Sufis were a mystical sect within the Muslims who flourished centuries ago. You have heard of the whirling dervishes, the ones who dance in circles? They come from that tradition. But it's the Sufi poets Hafiz and Rumi from the thirteenth and fourteenth centuries that I find so interesting. Here are a few sayings from each.

Hafiz wrote:

"I am a hole in the flute
 which Christ's breath moves through.
 Listen to this music."

and

"There are so many gifts
still unopened from your birthday.
There are so many handcrafted presents
 that have been sent to you by God."

and

"It is a great injustice and a monumental act of cruelty
 for any religion to make someone
 fear God."

Rumi wrote:

 "I called through your door,
'come out, the mystics are gathering in the streets.'
 'Go away, I'm sick.'
'I don't care if you're dying;
Jesus is here and he wants to resurrect somebody.'"

and

"In your Presence I don't want what I thought I wanted."

and

"Listen to me for one moment: quit being sad. Hear blessings dropping
their blossoms around you.—God."

There are many gifts of the Spirit, and they can be found in many places.
We, the people of the Spirit, should rejoice in them wherever they are found.

# Zora Neale Hurston

The first time that I saw Zora Neale Hurston she was coming down the sidewalk in Eau Gallie, Florida, jaunty and breezy, calling out to my mother-in-law with a loud voice, "Good mornin', Owen!" "Mornin', Zora. The coffee is on the stove; go in and help yourself." My mother-in-law introduced us, and Zora went in the house. We went on doing whatever it was we were doing.

Though I met Zora Neale Hurston that morning in the early 1950s, the name didn't mean anything more than it was her name and she was a friend of my mother-in-law.

I can't remember how many years later that I learned the identity of Mom's friend. She was ZORA NEALE HURSTON, black anthropologist, folklorist, writer, participant in the Harlem Renaissance, and friend to many literary people of the twenties and thirties. What was she doing in Eau Gallie, a small, unpretentious town? And how did she and Mom become such good friends?

By the time I had learned of Zora's work and accomplishments, she had moved on. No one knew where.

I asked Mom to tell me what she could about her friend. Did she know that she was a writer and anthropologist and had participated in a significant artistic movement? She knew a little bit about it but not much. Zora had given her one of her books and put an inscription in it for her. Sometimes Zora talked about those things but not a lot. Anyway, that wasn't what made them friends.

It was their friendship that was intriguing to me, knowing my mother-in-law as I did and getting to know Zora through her books and books about her.

Perhaps I should tell you how it all began. They met in Eau Gallie, a now non-existent town, having been swallowed up by the city of Melbourne. Mom was there because her husband was the depot agent for the Florida East Coast railroad. Zora was there because she had found a small cottage in 1929 near the depot and gathered together the research she had done on black life in the lumber camps and phosphate mines of central Florida. The material later became the book *Mules and Men*. She had come back to that very same place in the early 50s. Why, no one knows. Her sister-in-law said of her, "She moved every time you turned, and she'd been everywhere."

One day, Zora stopped down by the depot and asked the agent if he could help her to locate a trunk. She had been down in the West Indies studying the life and lore of Caribbean people. The trunk, with much of her material, was left in storage. Not having the money to reclaim it earlier, she was hoping now to find it.

It was that missing trunk that brought Mom into the picture. And here I must stop to tell you that Mom's sense of right and wrong, justice and injustice would qualify her as an Old Testament prophet. The trunk must be found! Sadly, it wasn't. Dad explained that after unclaimed baggage had been kept for so long, it was sold for a pittance. That's one of two times I know of that Zora's work was destroyed. After her death in 1960, her welfare home was cleaned out and papers burned.

The search for the trunk brought the two women together and started the friendship. I think they saw some similar life experiences and traits in common that each admired in the other, though as far as I know, they didn't say much about it to one another or to anyone else.

Both were born within 50 miles of each other at the turn of the century. Each had lost her mother at an early age. For Mom, it meant becoming mother to four younger siblings. For Zora, it was a stepmother whom she didn't like and living in a home where she didn't feel welcome. Both had to give up their schooling that they loved. These experiences made them very strong and very determined. Problems and difficulties were just things to face and overcome. Self-respect and pride in one's heritage were important and must be maintained. Both believed: don't let anything take control of you; you take control of it. No complaints, no regrets, keep pursuing the education that you didn't get.

One day, I was reading something Zora wrote about the subtle way that white people reveal their stereotypical views about black people. "Uh, oh," I thought, "she's talking about my mother-in-law now." Of course, that was before she met Mom, but it still applied.

I must stop and tell you that my mother-in-law was not a racist if by that word is meant someone who thinks others are inferior, finds ways to express it, and is disrespectful or abusive—or, I might add, refuses to associate with people of color. However, she was born in a small, white Southern town where stereotypical attitudes toward black people were a norm and seldom challenged. This was true of much of the South at the turn of the century.

She overcame many of these things by a fierce sense of fairness for all, great indignation, which called for action for anyone abused, and a deep concern for anyone sick, hungry, or homeless. She didn't just feel bad about things like that; she did something about it. Such things clearly and demonstrably shone through her formerly segregated upbringing.

Zora's color had nothing to do with the search for the missing trunk, morning visits, or daily coffee. Mom said that she soon realized Zora was very poor, but poor people were never treated as poor in her house, nor were rich treated as rich. Equality and courtesy for all was the household standard. Nevertheless, Zora couldn't help but see now and then some of those things segregated Southerners carried with them, whether they meant to or not. But Zora saw much more in her friend than the occasional, unintended sense of racial difference.

The friendship lasted for six years, and I don't know much of what each did for the other during that time. I know that Mom insisted, over some objection, that her friend Zora have a part in the PTA program at the local high school. That was a first for the all-white segregated school. I know that Zora campaigned in 1954 for Mom to be "Mother of the Year" and wrote numerous letters on her behalf. Mom wasn't chosen but received some kind of honorable mention. When it was all over, Zora must have given all the correspondence to her, for it was found among Mom's things when she died.

To the President of the Eau Gallie Woman's Club, Zora wrote:

"I suggest Mrs. Harry A. Owen for the distinction of MOTHER OF THE YEAR because of scope. After long and intimate association and observation, I can think of no other individual who so closely expressed the concept of the three hundred and sixty degrees of the circle. As you know, the capacity of an individual can only be expressed by the dimension of their mental and spiritual horizon. With some, the size of a thimble could enclose their concept of the universe, while to others, limitless space is hardly sufficient. Their eager, searching minds stretch out in an eternal searching and seeking hungrily. Mrs. Owen definitely belongs to the latter class. Without this hunger, this everlasting quest for more knowledge, more seeking after expressions of knowledge and ways of searching out means of expressing beauty and fullness of life, there is no advancement of civilization.

Mrs. Owen is forever discovering room for improvement in her own mind, in that of her children and in the social order of our time. Life did not grant her the opportunity of a college education, but she has striven to make up for it by intensive reading of good literature, what was available to her in adult education at the University of Florida, art expressions in music, ceramics, botany and home decoration, and legislation to improve social conditions. The interests of her children spread out in every direction like the rays from the rising sun. One famous educator has said that the measure of a man's success is not the point at which he arrived, but the place from which he started. Beginning at a place far down economically, Mrs. Owen has achieved wonders."

To son, Gene, she wrote:

"Did you ever hear a good old-time Baptist Negro giving God a good praying-over? Well, this is a mild sort of sample.

O, Lawd, here I is with my heart beneath my knees, and my knees in some lonesome valley, crying for mercy whilst mercy canst be found. . .please, PLEASE, my high-riding, my conquering King, come with peace in one hand and pardon in the other and be SO pleased in your tender mercy as to grant me one more favor whilst I'm still on pleading terms with mercy, and the blood still runs warm in my veins, to let these golden moments roll on a few years longer and grant to me. . .

So, (in time) this brings me us to the reason for my writing you this letter. To my way of thinking, if justice plumbs the line, your mother should be awarded the honor of MOTHER OF THE YEAR, that's the very corn I aim to grind. I can think of no mother in the nation who deserves it more than she.

From what I can glean about the procedure, the first thing is some expression of appreciation from the children of the proposed candidate. And, (to quote again), 'that is just what goodness I'm begging Righteousness to do.' If you will grant me this favor, I will be no further trouble to you.'"

To the younger son, Graham, she wrote:

"Doubtless numerous people who know your family well over this dangling peninsular will agree that your mother deserves to be named MOTHER OF THE YEAR. That is my conviction and so I am trying to do something about it. From what I have been able to learn about the procedure, it appears that the committee begins with expressions of appreciation from the offspring of the candidate. I need something of that sort from all seven of you. Recognition and acknowledgement of something more than the ordinary in the character of the mother. Perhaps your adjustment to your present situation might have come out of her example of accepting the handicaps of life and finding some way to bend them, for example. Her philosophy might be to urge her children to be such fighting dogs that your hides are worth money. (You know that certain states pay a bounty on grizzlies, mountain lions and timber wolves.) Courage, Invictus, and things like that might have come to you from your mother."

Both women moved away from Eau Gallie in the late 50s and lost touch with each other. Once, Mom went back to look for Zora but couldn't find her. Zora died in Fort Pierce, Florida in 1960 and was placed in a pauper's grave with no headstone. Mom went down there to find her grave but couldn't. Alice Walker tells of finding it in 1973 and placing a marker where it may be.

In *Dust Tracks on the Road*, Zora's autobiography, she said, "who can know the outer ranges of friendship? I am tempted to say no one can live without it. It seems to me trying to live without friends is like milking a goat to get cream for your morning coffee. It is a whole lot of trouble and then not worth much after you get it" (248).

# *Wanting New Rules*

A pastor friend was telling me about a group from his congregation who were leaving to start their own church. "Why would they want to do that?" I asked. "They are looking for a God with a different set of rules," he replied. In this case, their desire was to have a segregated church.

Looking for a God with a different set of rules is not peculiar to that group. It's common for all of us. My first question in facing a conflicting decision is to ask what I think and how I feel about the issue. That's not a sin but how much better to ask, "Lord, what would you have me do?" And, if Christ truly is Lord of life, I must, before the final decision is made, place it before Him.

Since I seldom get direct answers to such questions, prayer, thought, and struggle are often required. I suspect part of the struggle is between what I want and what God wants. To seek guidance and to follow it when found gives both clarity and determination and a strong sense of self control—gifts that are given when you follow God's direction.

In answer to a controversial question in the church, a man said to me, "As far as I'm concerned, I don't like it, but I believe that's what God wants done, and I'm going to do it." That's living by God's rule.

# *Pool Shark*

I had a high school buddy who was a pool shark. That is, he was an expert at pocket billiards. He introduced me to pool halls though I never came anywhere near his expertise. Two things I remember well: there was a heavy cloud of cigarette smoke that hung over the room, and every wall had at least one sign that said, "Keep One Foot On The Floor." What that admonition meant was that you could lean over the table as far as you could reach, but one foot must remain on the floor. The sign also forbade sitting on the table in a way that both feet were off the floor.

For some reason, that instruction remained with me, and when I entered the seminary, I transferred it over to theological advice. And this, of course, will need some explanation.

Religion comes from the world of mystery. It believes in an unseen God who does unseen things in a material world among physical beings. One of the first questions that we ask then is, "How do we get from here to there? And how are we to understand the words of an unseen God in a world of sight and sound?"

Long before the measuring of time and the effort to record the activities of human beings, archaeologists have found evidence of early humans' efforts to probe this mystery and understand its message. All kinds of religious systems have been devised and instructions given on how to understand and live in harmony with this unseen God. And how are we going to make our way through them to meet and possibly understand the God who is? This question made me remember the sign on the pool hall wall: Keep one foot on the floor! Though God is a mystery, this material world and physical body are what we were given to reflect His creative power and will. It is in this world that we are to live and serve God. It is to each other that we are to pass on His gifts.

The next time that you run into some uncertain notion about God, trust your common sense and stay grounded, which in pool hall parlance means, "Keep one foot on the floor."

Two things in closing: The best way I know to find God (note: I did not say only) is through the life and love and teachings of Jesus. And secondly, though we think we are looking for God, it is God who is so much more looking for us.

# *Human Rights for All*

The rights of homosexual and transgender people have been much in the news lately, and since the Supreme Court has recognized the right of same-sex couples to marry, it has come even closer to our attention and, in a way, forced us to examine ourselves and our social groups to ask how inclusive or exclusive we are towards these groups.

As this issue confronts the Christian church, it has caused many to open their doors wider in welcome and others to close theirs more tightly. Recently, I was asked, as a minister, to share my thoughts, and here is what I said:

The reason I cannot single out any person or persons from the church is because the first time I do this, I exclude myself. The decision as to who is acceptable is up to God, not me. The God I know and love has issued an invitation that says, "Whosoever will may come" and "Come unto me, all of you who labor and are heavy laden. . ." It is an invitation of graceful love issued to everyone. It is not mine to give or take away.

I am aware that the Bible, especially the Old Testament, has strong condemnation of homosexual behavior, even calling for death, and, if you want to find some "proof texts," you can. However, that was thousands of years ago when they knew nothing about genetics and gender differences or the wide spectrum of human sexuality. They only knew male and female and the strict regulations as to how they believed each should act. I have no desire to adhere to all of their rules nor to reach back and select a few that I wish to enforce in the 21st century. Christianity comes from ancient Judaism, and much of it is to be admired, but a lot of it has to do with the ethnicity of those people and does not universally apply. In fact, Jesus often disregarded many of these things in the face of human need such as the case of the woman with a bleeding condition (Luke 8: 43-45). His invitation was always, "Come as you are: God loves you, forgives you, and accepts you."

The radicalness of Jesus and the New Testament message is that God loves all of us unconditionally, especially those who have been rejected or excluded. The teaching of the New Testament is that we are all flawed human beings and that God's love and grace are freely given to all to bring us into the fullness of the life we have each been given.

As to questions of gender and sexuality, we tend to think of them in either

166

or terms when in reality they are more on a spectrum and we can fall along it with no choice of our own.

Cultures and societies have always made decisions about who is acceptable and who is not, and churches are in danger of doing the same thing. However, in my opinion, if we are true to our faith, it is come one, come all!

# *False Advertising*

One of my pet peeves is religious advertising. The Sunday paper usually has the most of them, and the majority come from those home grown sects that got their start here in the U.S. They are the ones who announce MIRACLE HEALINGS! PROPHECIES EXPLAINED! THE END IS NEAR; COME AND BE READY!

It's not the variety of churches that bother me; it's the variety of claims that some make, implying they have the whole truth while others don't or that they can heal or prophesy the future, etc. Finding an understandable and acceptable religious faith for yourself may not be easy at best, but it is made more difficult by claims such as these.

The Apostle Paul ran into this problem at the church in Corinth. They seemed quite pleased with their many demonstrations of faith as well as the people who led them to Christianity, such as Peter, Paul, and Apollos. None of these people are that important, Paul said, and went on to list a number of spiritual gifts they seemed proud of. At the end of the list, he said, "But I will show you a more excellent way. . ." Here he began the great love chapter, I Corinthians 13, which ends with "So faith, hope and love abide; these three; but the greatest of these is love."

Wouldn't it be wonderful if some Sunday all of the churches on the religious page took out one large ad that read COME SHARE FAITH, HOPE, AND LOVE WITH ANY OR ALL OF US! If that happens, I'll try my hand at prophecy: The kingdom of God will have come on earth!

# *Avoiding Cynicism*

My first assignment as a pastor was to a small Florida town located on U.S. Highway 19, one of the two major roadways at that time that brought people into the state. The Methodist parsonage wasn't twenty feet from the highway, and we could see everything that came and went from our front door. One thing I wasn't prepared for was the flood of people who came down this road when fall turned to winter up north. "Snow Birds" the Florida folk called them and there were many. Along with them came a number of vagrant travelers, and they were numerous too. Somehow, these folk all managed to land at our front door and, oddly enough, were Methodists, or so they said.

Being a young pastor and full of idealism, I felt I must treat each as an honored guest and help as much as I could. But after numerous visits and similar stories that left them at my front door without help unless provided by me, I became suspicious and a bit cynical. That's when I began to try to get at the "real" story to see if anything could be done there. (I gave this up sometime later. They were smarter than I and better story tellers.)

One night a tall, gangly man knocked at the door and asked if he could talk with the pastor. I invited him in, and he began to tell me a sad story of a wife and six children in Pensacola. He had gone to south Florida seeking work and not finding any was trying to get back home. As he told his story, large tears rolled down his cheeks and dripped on his shirt. The story was so touching I began to get a lump in my throat when something said, "It can't be true! It's just too sad. He's made it all up to get my sympathy." I remembered he had said he was Catholic, so I asked the name of his parish.

"St. Michael's" he replied.

"And who is your priest?"

"Father Paul Hogarty."

"Both of those names sounded Catholic," I said to myself. "He's pretty good at this."

"If I were your priest," I told him, "I would want to know that you were having difficulty getting home. I'll give Father Hogarty a call and let him know you are here."

I didn't expect the operator to give me a number for St. Michael's parish, but she did, and, when I asked for Father Hogarty, he came to the phone. "Everything he told you is true", he said, "and if you made him walk home it wouldn't help. We look after his family the best we can. If you will help him get home, I'll return the money to you." We argued over the cost of his return and finally agreed to divide it between us.

I felt a tinge of guilt the next morning when I wrote Father Hogarty and tried to explain my cynicism as best I could. I remember saying I didn't like being a sucker for a soft touch. A few days later,I received the following letter:

Dear Reverend Zimmerman:

The kindness you have extended to our parishioner is truly appreciated. But not this only. I am most grateful in your considerateness in consulting us..

Our Lord is certainly pleased when whatever is done is positive proof of love for Him. Please don't be discouraged by the soft touch. It's always the Magdalene chance to anoint His feet that the Judas thriftiness would rationalize better. Don't be discouraged!

And how good it would be to hear at our judgment in contrast to all else, .."but for the poor he had a soft touch!"

Do continue by the faith you have in the Master. I, the man, am fool without a doubt, but it is never when I am following Christ, however it may seem. Be encouraged my brother; our faith is not in vain.

The humor and sport you have evidenced is ample assurance that you are well accustomed to the stride of Our Master's steps. I am so delighted.

AD MULTOS ANNOS!

Father Paul Hogarty

# *Marriage Equality*

Why did I perform a gay marriage ceremony? I do not think homosexuality is a personal choice any more than being male or female. Our gender is a result of God's creative process.

Within the history of humankind, there is a tendency to set other groups apart as different than we and less than we are. We then denigrate them because of that difference, be it color, language, custom, or gender. Once devalued, they become diminished, abused, and even enslaved. Such is the history of slavery in many cultures. Such is the abuse of homosexuals.

It is very clear that Jesus did not devalue anyone. The last shall be first, He said. We are to seek out the lost and least and tell them how loved and valued they are by God.

I am a minister of the Gospel. How can I refuse to take part in a wedding service of a dear friend who is one of the most faithful and valued members of our church?

Why must homosexuals have to hide what they consider their basic identity in order to be accepted by general society and sometimes their own family and friends?

I have often thought of the anguish that youth go through when discovering their affinity for the same sex. A niece shared all this with me before she went home to tell her parents, and I had a glimpse into her struggle and pain.

On June 12, 2016, those of us who live here in Orlando awoke to a newspaper headline that said the deadliest mass shooting in recent history had taken place here during the night; 49 people were killed and more than 50 injured. This was at the Pulse nightclub not far from our home. The shooter had been raised by his father to hate gay people. This is the final result of such hatred.

I have no special expertise or insight into human sexuality. I just can't believe that God made a mistake when some humans find themselves physically attracted to their same sex.

# *Singing the Wondrous Story*

Softly quoting the words of the song, she said, "Do you know that 'ymn? Hi forget the name, but it's number 380 in your 'ymnal, the fourth werse." I thought a moment and said, "Yes, I know it. It's called 'Let Us Sing the Wondrous Story.'"

We'd been waiting a long time, three hours at least, waiting for the surgeon to come tell us if her daughter was alright and, if she were, how much longer could she live after the operation. Behind those three hours were nine weeks in a Nassau hospital and beyond that as many more in a little out-island settlement with a sick child.

I kept saying to myself, "Lord, let her live. Let her live for the sake of this good woman, if for no one else," but the symptoms didn't sound good, and the doctor had made some guarded statements about her recovery.

"When 'e comes you ask 'im about it," she said. "Hi don't think hi could hear the news." When the doctor came, he said the little girl had come through the surgery alright but the tumor had spread too far.

The fourth verse of hymn 380 in her hymnal says:

"Days of Darkness still come o'er me;
Sorrow's paths I often tread:
But the Savior still is with me,
By his hand I'm safely led."

Please, dear God, let it be so.

# A Friend with God

Since I was a small child, I have felt some kind of friendly relationship with God. Note I did not say I "believed" in God. Believing in something and feeling related to it are two different things. Anyway, I think I was too young to have "beliefs." In the same way, I felt related to and close to my parents, I felt related and close to God. "Of course," I hear someone say, "most all children do." If they do or don't, the purpose of this article is to say, I still do.

My grandfather had a small farm at the edge of town, and, in the midst of the Depression, our family moved to the farm. Frankly, I thought it was better than city living. We had a cow and chickens and all kinds of wonderful vegetables. We had a pony and a fish pond. Who could want more?

The only thing we didn't have for the first year or two was electricity. Even so, I didn't mind it that much. In fact, I liked to be able to walk outside of the house and see the night sky undiluted by house lights or street lamps. It gave me a sense of awe about God's creative power. It's interesting that though I was staring out into infinity, God still seemed very near.

A few years after the farm, we moved to the small coastal town of Crystal Beach. That, too, was a joyful place for a boy to grow up. My father built us a "skiff" ( a small boat for rowing or poling), and I was on the water as much as the land. Once again, I felt that sense of familiarity and closeness to God,

I joined the Navy in WWII and wherever I was sent, continued to pray to my friend I knew at the farm and my companion on the bay.

I had no plans to become a minister. The war years increased my determination to live the Christian life but no thoughts of entering the ministry. Suffice it to say I did, which required several years of study of the Bible and Theology and after that lectures and the latest books on religion. Even so, I never felt I understood everything or had it all put together.

Lately, I've been thinking I would like to go fishing one more time with my friend God or stand out in the darkness with Him again and say, "Wow, look what you've done!" I've read all the books about Him that I want. I'd just like for us to do something fun together.

# An Exchange of Wit

I have a dear friend who used to call and say, "Let's get together for an exchange of wit and a flow of soul." It was an interesting remark, and I never forgot it, but lately his words began to have a lot more meaning.

I live in a retirement center, and every evening I would walk past an old friend and former church member. You don't just walk past old friends, so each evening I paused a moment for an " exchange of wit." It was mostly bantering back and forth about football or golf or something going on in town. We were both Florida "Crackers" too. (Which means we were born and grew up here before the tourists started staying year round.) This heritage gave us a sense of connection.

My friend died this week, and his family asked that I speak at his service. That's when I began to realize our casual meeting each evening was more than just an "exchange of wit." It was also a "flow of soul;" something passed between us in those few moments that left its imprint on each of us. I don't quite know how to explain this, but when you are positively engaged with someone, even a stranger, something good is given and passes between you and leaves its mark.

For example, when you ask a stranger for directions and he stops what he is doing to give you the information, something good is happening between you; he is giving you his time and knowledge, and you are experiencing a spirit of gratitude for his gift. That is when a "flow of soul" takes place; something of a good and helpful nature has passed between you. This is just a minor example; it happens all the time between family members and old friends all who remain lovingly open to each other.

I got lost last week. I thought I knew just where I was going but didn't. Finally, I stopped at a jewelry store to ask for information. The young lady I asked didn't know the location I was looking for but stopped what she was doing and began to search for it. She then called her manager who came out with a smile and told me where it was and how to get there.

I doubt that either of them thought they were doing something unusual, but, in the warmest and most friendly way and at a momentary cost of their time (which had nothing to do with the jewelry business), stopped to help me find my way. To me, it was that "flow of soul," that cheerful sharing of oneself to help another.

As for an "exchange of wit," I promised if ever I got married again (we are currently in our sixty seventh year), I would certainly come there to buy the ring.

# *Thank You*

I recently read a statement on prayer by Meister Eckhart, a mystic-theologian from the Middle Ages. It was so simple it's hard to believe, yet I do and try to practice it. But before we get to his comment on prayer, I'd like to share a few thoughts about it.

I think many people do not pray because they don't know how to start or what to say in their own words. Also, they hear a prayer language in Church that isn't part of their own vocabulary. The preachers often use it but with stilted words or a holy tone that the laity don't know how to speak or, maybe, don't want to. So now's the time to tell you what Meister Eckhart said: "IF THE ONLY PRAYER WE EVER SAY IN OUR LIVES IS THANK YOU, THAT WILL BE ENOUGH."

What? No thees or thous, nor "We are not worthy so much as to gather up the crumbs under thy table?"

Just thank you will do? Yes, I think he's right. In fact, I've been praying that way for some time, only I say "yes" and "thank you." This calls for some explanation, so I will tell you what these words mean to me.

To pray at all means you are addressing Someone. It means you believe there is a Creative Power or Presence that is the Source of our being. You may be very uncertain or unsure, but to simply say "thank you" is to take you a step beyond those doubts. And when you do it often enough, a sense of gratitude begins to build for all those people and places and events for which you gave thanks. You begin to realize how gifted you are for your spouse, your children, this community and nation, and a multitude of others things that enrich your life.

The One we are thanking will always remain a mystery to us, but, for me, the words of Jesus are enough: "If you've seen me you've seen the Father." Translated: If you know what Jesus is like, you know what God is like. WOW! That means a bit of the Creator's beauty has shown in the life of Jesus and revealed itself to us and this is the One who is listening. THANK YOU! THANK YOU! THANK YOU!

And what about the "yes" I add to my prayer? It is to say to the God who acts like Jesus, "If there's anything I can do for you, the answer is 'Yes.'"

If you are one of those persons who has trouble praying, just start saying "Thank You" for all those people and places and things that are blessing your life. You will discover how much pleasure it is to pray. And maybe you'll even